Discovering Your True Brilliance

Discovering Your True Brilliance

How to Let your Radiance Shine Through on the Path to Awareness and Transformation

Sheila Giardina

BALBOA.
PRESS

A DIVISION OF HAY HOUSE

Balboa Press books may be ordered through booksellers or by contacting:

Balboa Press
A Division of Hay House
1663 Liberty Drive
Bloomington, IN 47403
www.balboapress.com
1-(877) 407-4847

Because of the dynamic nature of the Internet, any web addresses or links contained in this book may have changed since publication and may no longer be valid. The views expressed in this work are solely those of the author and do not necessarily reflect the views of the publisher, and the publisher hereby disclaims any responsibility for them.

The author of this book does not dispense medical advice or prescribe the use of any technique as a form of treatment for physical, emotional, or medical problems without the advice of a physician, either directly or indirectly. The intent of the author is only to offer information of a general nature to help you in your quest for emotional and spiritual well-being. In the event you use any of the information in this book for yourself, which is your constitutional right, the author and the publisher assume no responsibility for your actions.

Any people depicted in stock imagery provided by Thinkstock are models, and such images are being used for illustrative purposes only.
Certain stock imagery © Thinkstock.

Printed in the United States of America

ISBN: 978-1-4525-6884-3 (sc)
ISBN: 978-1-4525-6886-7 (hc)
ISBN: 978-1-4525-6885-0 (e)

Library of Congress Control Number: 2013902905

Balboa Press rev. date: 2/22/2013

TABLE OF CONTENTS

Editor's Note: *Sheila is also called Sheshe because her grandchildren could not pronounce Sheila and Sheshe was easier. Now most of the people in her life also call her Sheshe.*

Forward:
Sandy Jiggy Lembke

I met Sheila in 2008 when I was playing an online gaming site. This was something I used to fill my time after losing my mom the previous year. Mom's passing was devastating; she was my best friend, and we did everything together. When I look back at myself during that timeframe, I was a very depressed, bitter person with no self-esteem, a bad attitude, just trying to get through the day. Although I had a few close friends, I pretty much disliked people. It was easier for me to have a crappy attitude, then to have a conversation with someone. Where I lived I never spoke to my neighbors' or anyone outside my small circle of comfort.

When I started playing on this gaming site, I just wanted to play my games and be left alone. It was so out of character to reach out to anyone, but I did reach out to Sheila and I was completely amazed at how my relationship with her blossomed. There was an instant connection. Soon I learned that just about everyone who encounters Sheila sees her bright light as she makes people feel good. Everyone calls her Sheshe because her grandchildren could only say Sheshe and it has stuck. Loving her like a mom, I know now that God had a hand in our coming together.

We started out chatting through Yahoo Messenger, where she would share with me some of her 'tools' to help me feel better about myself. Then in April of 2009, I went into her website, ShesheMiracles. com. At the time, I still had my "whatever" attitude, yet still enjoyed talking to her, so I decided to just go along with it. Never, never in a million years, did I believe that any of it was going to be making a difference in my life. Slowly, I started to notice little changes in myself. I started to believe in me and oh boy have I been on an incredible journey these past two years!

After using Sheshe's 'tools' for about a year, I had a desire to meet her; even though she lived six hours north of me. I had never gone further than my hometown, never on the freeways. This combined with low finances; I figured it was impossible for me to get there. Then, all of a sudden, all these little things started happening. I received unexpected income; my husband repaired the truck, things started to fall into place. Sure enough, in a matter of one week of putting out that desire, I was on my way to San Jose with my three children to spend Easter with people I had never met before. I was going to be meeting Sheshe, her family and friends. This was really big for me, remember, I was still afraid of people at that point. We spent four days at Sheshe's home and she worked with not only me but my children as well. On the way back home, the children were completely different, they were being kind and loving with each other; and were sharing and being polite.

Since that first trip, I have been back to Sheshe's home about six times in two year. The last three trips were to help Sheshe get this book together. In this past year, I have opened up so much.

My kids and I have a closeness that I never believed would have been possible. They are starting to believe that they are in control of their lives, and that attitude is everything. Sheshe has taught me to love, to have faith, to forgive, to be grateful, to see beauty and to believe in miracles. Once I started to be grateful, miracles started coming in abundance. Sheshe's program also helped me discover my passion; I never believed I had a passion for anything. Boy was I wrong! It's funny how things unfold when you are open and grateful. So many times, I have had exactly what I needed, it's like magic.

Sheshe and I did a prayer for the new neighbors that would be moving in next door to me, and a week later, the most amazing couple, Joan and Bill, moved in. Now remember, I had lived in my home for about eight years and I never spoke to any of my neighbors. One day, shortly after Joan and Bill moved in, I was out gardening. This was another first for me and Sheila taught me how. Joan called over and asked me "You like antiques don't you", which of course I did. Joan asked if I would like some furniture she no longer wanted. I had just been telling Sheshe I needed some new furniture.

The next day I found myself on craigslist looking for a couch. The very next day, another neighbor came over to tell me that there was some furniture out on a driveway of an elderly neighbor, and I was welcome to go help myself. I walked over to the neighbor's and sitting there was an almost brand new couch, exactly the style I was looking for. It did not stop there, more vintage and antique furniture, also known as shabby chic, started coming my way. Joan, who sells shabby chic furniture, was amazed and asked me to start selling with her. Joan bought a shop and I have been working with her for the last six months and love it.

Since then, I have found that I am passionate about buying, fixing up, and selling furniture. I am in heaven, and with my faith and positive attitude, and the universe brings me what I need. I am blessed and these tools work miracles. Watching miracles over and over again brings me joy as I was the biggest non-believer there was. Every day I am amazed at what a different person I am because of Sheshe and her 'tools'.

It has been an honor for me to help put her work together into this book. Sheila has an incredible gift, selflessly touching many lives, and her desire is to touch many more. Sheila's program is so powerful that when we started working on the book, our lives started taking off at an amazing speed. I personally found that the "me" I have been working on suddenly woke up and got it! I believe in this program, I know it works, and I will continue to use these tools, and share them wherever I can. I now even have a long-range goal to develop the Sandy style of shabby chic furnishings.

ACKNOWLEDGMENTS

This book is dedicated to my family. Without them, I would have not have desired to look within myself and become a better person. To my grandchildren, may they know how to blow up their balloons of self-esteem.

This book took an extended time to put together, and there are many people who helped me craft this non-fiction work.

I say craft because collecting stories discovered in my journals while reviewing and re-read them is the basis for *Discovering Your True Brilliance.*

My friends encouraged, supported my dreams and deserve credit and thanks for helping me. Some of them provided feedback on stories and letters expressing how this process worked in their life.

****

Lynn Rogers taught me that women have just as much power as men throughout generations, which allows me to know I can fly.

I have been so blessed to have help from others to see this work completed. Starting with the people who believed it was worth a try.

Thank you to Joyce Sinclair, who helped develop an outline for a workbook *Discovering Your Brilliance* I self-published in 2004.

To the first Power Circle of friends who learned with me and saw answered prayers show up. All of you who believed in me as I searched for my spiritual path and participated in my first Power Circle: Nancy, B.J., Trish, Cathy, Diana, Doreen, Aram, Sandy, and Toni – I Thank You!

To B.J. King for magically bringing my words and intentions into a flowing read. Her patience, tactful criticism, determination and prayers helped us as we pulled this book together.

To Sandy Lembke for her willingness to read all my writings over and over again. For her commitment in driving seven hours to come help me in any way, twice a year. I am a healthier person because of giving me her time with the book and the website. Thank you for writing the introduction to the book, you said it so beautifully from the heart.

To Diana Witherington, for flying from Alabama to California to my home and giving the tools a go. She found her "Knight in Shining Armor".

For my Daughter Billie Jo Periman and her soul mate, for believing this process could save their marriage and it did.

To Cindy Krause who came to me looking for a job as a teacher after being out of work for two years. She began helping to edit the book and two weeks later, she found her dream job. Answered Prayer.

To Patrick Lynch for taking time out of his busy schedule to shoot my cover photo on short notice.

To all you who read and use the tools to *Discovering Your True Brilliance* will guide you to be the best you possible.

A grateful Thank You to Authors such as Wayne Dwyer, Marianne Williamson, Iylana Vanzant, Louise Hay, Dr. Norman Vincent Peale, Anthony Robbins, M. Scott Peck, Neale Donald Walsch, and too many more to name that have come before me and been my inspirational healers.

Sheila Wants You To Know…

Discovering Your True Brilliance is my personal journey of healing and transformation to live the most positive life that I can. The idea was to share the tools and thoughts that have worked for me, my friends, family and even the children in my life.

Too many of us avoid opportunities to fertilize our qualities. I call it 'self- fertilization' or to make productive. As we nurture ourselves as often as possible, we become stronger, reliable and patient. This process is needed as much as breathing, exercising, eating and taking care of our everyday needs. It is also a way of maintaining and discovering our true abilities.

Our imagination is a powerful gift, creating a positive mental system to nurture our desires. It is important to teach ourselves to think and focus on being in the present.

Starting from this moment, know all things are possible. It is with this open mindedness that you allow a miracle to transport its gift to you. When you focus on past experiences, you waste precious moments waiting for a better outcome.

When something happens that looks to be negative, stop your mind games from reflecting on the negative and look forward to a great life. I love this saying: "If it doesn't look good, God is not in it, bring God back into it and see God's miracles unfold". (I call my spiritual guide God, and please call your guide whatever is comfortable for you.)

Have you ever read a story that has several endings? That is how life is to me. Now when I find myself in a situation I do not desire, I have the choice to change the ending, or stay in the old story. Another quote that comes to mind, "If you always think, what you have always thought, you will always get what you have always got."

It is in our best interest to reach for a new and different ending to the old stories. You can choose a better outlook by telling yourself that a miracle is a good ending causing it to be a win-win for all. Just by filling our head with positive thoughts, we can be filled with wonderful opportunities.

Remember, you are the only one responsible for speaking the words that create your life.

What This Book Can Do For You–
B. J. King, Editor

The content in *Discovering Your True Brilliance* is nonfiction and compiled from 16 plus years of journal entries, stories, streams of consciousness, and conversations with friends and family. What is important is the content will provide a wonderful way to tackle life issues with greater ease and success.

Sheila, also known as Sheshe, not only transformed her life she continues to help hundreds of people in different parts of the world using these methods for well-being. Her goal was to create various tools that are easy to use and make dramatic differences in anyone's life.

At one time, Sheila lived in a sea of mixed messages leading to low self-esteem. There were times she just wanted to climb into bed hoping to never leave again. Sheila has told others, "I finally discovered what worked for me and it continually reminds me of who I really am and why I wanted to share these tools and techniques with you."

Throughout this book, Sheshe will share stories, thoughts, tips, tools, and miracles. At the end of each block of text will be blank spaces to jot down your thoughts and ideas. There are exercises for you to do alone or with others. However, doing these exercises alone, gives you, the opportunity to create quiet times allowing you to listen and tap into your inner thoughts and higher power. These times can spark enlightenment and possibilities. Listening to ourselves is also important in this process and allows us to focus. In addition there are games of support that will perk you up, and even reveal "ah-ha moments".

One more thing, at the end of some chapters and sections of the chapters are poems. Sheila began painting rocks with ladybugs and power words back in 2005. She attached a small card to the rock with a poem about the power words. Her goal was to get powerful messages out to people so she sold the rocks to raise money to print her first workbook. She also contributed funds to the Master Gardener program and the Heritage Rose Garden.

Now make yourself a pot of tea,
sit back, and relax while
DISCOVERING YOUR TRUE BRILLIANCE

PART 1

CHAPTER 1

THE FIRST BEGINNING – LIFE CHANGES

Editor's Note: *The following lessons from life tell the story of Sheila's early days through journal entries and streams of consciousness.*

Sheila grew up in a negative atmosphere. She would like people to understand the impact it has on children. There is no such thing as a little negative, it can sting as much as a big one.

Children and the Words They Hear–
Balloon Story

Negative words and messages blocked me for some forty-five years. I pray that no child has to wait that long to discover his/her brilliance! My Mother's Sister, Aunt Marie, was the one who gave me encouraging words to live a great life. She is in my heart now even though she is no longer with us, she now has her wings. The words she spoke to me were always positive. Those words are the ones that gave me the courage to become the person I am today.

Aunt Marie had that gift of always finding something good to share about what she saw in me. She taught me how to smile because she believed in me. She was pure love and always had a tinkle in her eyes. I could walk into any room that she was in and feel the heat from her love. Her intake of breath let me know I was the most important person to her. I found this true with all her friends as well, I always felt safe, welcomed and loved. Anytime I would need to uplift my spirits, I could imagine she was right in the room. I would imagine I had balloon's all around me filled with my hopes and dreams and that made me feel good. When I was around Aunt Marie all my balloons were flying high around me. Each lifted my spirit and built my self-esteem and I was so happy.

When I would hear a negative word I could imagine a pin hole in the balloon letting all the air out and it would land on the floor. Many days though, all the balloons were all over the floor. At home, when my parents bawled me out, I would run to my bedroom with all the crying drama. I would lie there and repeat all the verbal belittling words over and over in my head and cry. When I think back on it, I would always be the hardest on myself when my balloons would flatten. In time the balloons would just lie there because I was not be able to lift my spirits at all. Around the seventh grade my balloons were so out of air I became a magnet to boys whose balloons were also deflated and we came together to support each other, even if we didn't understand that is what we were doing. When I found I could feel real good with a boy, it became my greatest joy. I wanted that kind of attention, even if it came with their belittling remarks. I allowed it, because it was my normal.

I know if children had some positive words to fill their days, it would open them up and allow good and wonderful things to come, early in life. Having a positive person say one sentence to a child empowers them and is a gift for a lifetime. So I thought, what could thirty minutes of all positive words a day do for a child or even an adult? I believed it would give them strength and courage to handle challenges. Having positive affirmations to use would make the difference in the world and replace the negative words said to them. Children are the most honest people I have encountered. They are born believing the best about themselves and others. On their arrival, they come into this world to a party filled with hopes and dreams. With balloons all around them, called "Happy Balloons." As our children grow, someone may come along with negative words, and pop a balloon with a sentence like:

"You can't do that! Pop!

"You will break that!" Pop!

"You don't know how!" Pop!

"You can't do anything right!" Pop!

"Who do you think you are?" Pop!

After I gave birth to my daughter, the cycle of mixed messages started again. I could only pass on what I had learned and heard.

So when my Daughter tried something I felt she should not be doing, I turned to the only words and actions I knew. "Bad baby"! Pop! Don't do that! Pop!

Don't touch that! Pop! Her balloons began to fall down around her and land on the floor. I believed the messages I was given were the truth about me, and they followed me into adulthood. I was causing her the pain that I experienced; I had forgotten how powerful Aunt Marie's positive words helped me, so why not my children.

Showing others how to bring positive words into their lives gives me a feeling of knowing children can blow up their balloons when needed. With positive guidance and words of encouragement, children will make better choices in their lives, and so can you.

Thank you Aunt Marie for showing me how to blow up my balloons.

Lessons From Life

I was born in San Francisco, CA. in 1949 and my parents divorced before I was two years old. My mother had to work, so I was boarded out to live with a lady who taught ballet and tap. I lived with this teacher for about two years. Mother did not know the lady's brother was the neighborhood pimp, now known as a pedophile. During those two years I was violated time and time again, not only by him but his friends as well. There was no one to tell because of being threatened and frightened. The messages from those men were not the same as most little girls would receive from people who love them. I was told I was such a good girl for the things I had to do with men.

I went back to my mother after she married my stepfather. Then the new messages began, these are the messages I overheard him tell my mother: "she won't amount to anything." "she is so stupid" "nobody's going to want her", "she belongs in reform school." What I was learning was "Life is the pits, and then it gets worse", on and on to the point believing it was so. These messages continued in my head long after these people's voice's were out of my thoughts. We moved to

Sacramento for a short time for a new start, and then to Capitola when I was in third grade.

My parents were good souls. They thought as so many other parents, that by pointing out my faults, they would try to change me. Not! Maybe if I had believed in myself more, there could have been more positive changes! Growing up, I had not been shown how to use my own brain or heart, there were no tools or words to use that would encourage me. The positive words from Aunt Marie were plowed under, showing up later to guide me.

I believed that what my parents told me was true. They were doing their best and their best was using what both of their parents had taught them. What is so important is to break the cycle of negative language and verbal abuse in our own lives and families.

PROMISCUOUS

I was promiscuous with Bob the first boy that asked. Pregnant with my first child at sixteen, Bob left me. My mother sent me to live with her sister Marie in Sacramento until they could decide what to do with me. We didn't have money for an unwed mothers home. One day I met a 21-year-old man named Jeff who really liked me. He asked my family if he could marry me 2 days after we met. They liked him and thought it was a good idea to get married and we set up home in Capitola. At first, I enjoyed being a wife, taking care of our apartment, and having dinner on the table. After a short time, he began raping and belittling me about everything. So many things began to happen all at once. One day, a woman came to the apartment when Jeff was at work and handed me papers he had filled out to put my baby up for adoption as soon as it was born. I told her no and made her leave. Then Jeff went away for a weekend and did not come home. I waited for six weeks and then I applied for welfare so I could eat and have a place to live for my daughter and me. I soon learned that he was in jail.

Within 18 months, I gave birth to a baby boy and now I was caring for two adorable children. I continued to be in and out of marriages and the next man I married had two small daughters who I ended up raising as my own. Soon I left him taking only the children and the clothes on our backs. The good news is he had moved us to San Jose where there was decent housing and jobs I could work even while on welfare. I seemed to always marry men who had low self- esteem just as I did.

Celebration Rock

"I AM ALIVE!

That is reason enough to celebrate"

Change Is Happening

The good news is I raised all 4 children by myself on welfare. My job as a waitress was fun because I loved making people happy serving their meals. Determined to make it on my own, I worked part-time while getting welfare to make ends meet. As the children grew, I would also clean homes with my friend who had her own house cleaning business. The children were growing up and I was feeling that we were doing just fine.

In time, I was able to give up waitressing and welfare and formed a small business called Old Fashion Quality Housekeeping. My clients were wonderful people and after the first 3 weeks, I would ask them for a letter of recommendation. It helped me feel I was doing a good job and was appreciated. My self-esteem and balloons were rising and I had more confidence in myself to be successful.

I had two other women who worked for me and would ask their clients to write recommendations for each of them. We all needed a boost and to know that we were appreciated. When we are appreciated, we always do a better job and go above and beyond what is normally expected. I was so proud of making $10,000 a year with my business, which was a lot for me to live on. When on welfare we only received about $6,000 a year and that was for four children and me.

After the children grew up and started out on their own, I rented a room from a friend, put everything into a storage shed, and started paying off my debts. In my forties, I began to understand what had happened all those years and was able to forgive others and especially myself.

My Freedom Rocks

"I celebrate the glory of Freedom.
I value my Freedom.
I share my Freedom.
I live in Freedom.
When I look at my Freedom Rock
I give thanks to all who have made
my freedom possible."

PART 2

Chapter 2

New Beginnings – 30 Years Later

Editor's Note: *It matters not how long it takes to change. What is most important is the recognition that change is needed. Have the determination and courage to save your own life is the first step toward a life of peace, love, joy, happiness, success and so much more. Finally making the changes necessary to show you can do anything once you set your mind to it is the second big step.*

Celebration

One day I made a list of the qualities I desired in a male friend, and taped the list on my TV to remind me at all times. Still renting a room from my girlfriend, I went back to bowling with my old league. This is where I met Ed who had the qualities I was looking for.

Ed and I were living together in 1992 when I fell down a flight of stairs while cleaning a house and broke my back. Being flat on my back for over a year, depression set in and surrounded me from all sides. My get up and go, got up and went and I wanted something, besides meds to wake me up so I could feel like living again. I wanted more energy and better health so I could be successful in my life. Having a purpose to get out of that bed, and believe in me again was my way out of depression. I heard about the importance of having high energy, so I began reading about how to develop high energy to find ways to help me accomplish my goals.

To keep my energy levels high, I felt I would have to stay positive. Being negative wasn't cutting it, and complaining seemed to be bringing me more negativity. I was never out of drama! Drama is addicting.

Ed took good care of me in spite of the drama during that time and oh by the way, Ed and I have been married over 20 years.

Wow Rock

"Something BIG
has happened in my world.
I stop asking "why?"
I now state "WOW"
I see this makes a difference
in my thinking and my being.
"WOW"

       LESSONS FROM LIFE

Finding Strength And Power

I needed to find strength in each situation I found myself. Telling myself there is a bigger picture than this broken back was helping me move into a more positive way of life. The time flat on my back did give me opportunity to be with myself, my thoughts, and to discover what my desires really were. In time, I came to believe breaking my back was the best thing that ever happened to me. It gave me the opportunity to do some soul searching and some major life adjustments. Discovering the power of positive thinking, I began writing down my inner thoughts. This is where I created the daily tools for my success, to keep me on my path, and to bring me up when I am down. Finding and using the tools religiously caused me to see miracles as prayers being answered. I was happy again, and with greater energy.

LESSONS FROM LIFE

Attitude

Part of the healing also dealt with my attitude and I learned there is truly an immense power in our attitude. I believe the events in my life related directly to my attitude and then I read these words: "The greatest discovery of my generation is that human beings can alter their lives simply by altering their attitude"

William James.

Understanding this has taught me to shape my life by developing a positive mental attitude, which in turn has created a positive life.

For years, I did not know what I wanted to do with myself. I only knew what I did not want, where I did not want to do it, and who I did not want in my life. For so many years living life from a negative perspective obviously produced negative results. Dreaming of being happy, I realized I was not. I was constantly searching in all the wrong places for my life's missing ingredients. My attitude for years led me to believe that life was the pits, and that was my truth, because believing made it so.

One day I asked myself, 'How exactly do I go about developing a positive mental attitude?' I already learned my thoughts determine what I say and do.

Thinking for myself, was the first act in creating my new world, and to stop being a robot that can only do as others instruct. I started to believe in myself, by monitoring and listening to my thoughts and questioning whether they were in my best interest or for my highest good. I continued to question everything I came into contact with, and that is how my learning takes place. The saying "If I always think, what I always thought, I will always get what I always got" is so true.

Soon, I discovered what I had been looking for and where to find it; the answers lay inside of me all along: a change of attitude.

Changing my attitude caused my life to change, giving me a new truth. Looking through dusty glasses is never really what it appears to be, life is so much more. Let us examine attitude more closely and see how we actually do control our lives by controlling what we think and how we think about it which takes us back to "We are what we think" .

The dictionary defines attitude as 'a state of mind or feeling with regard to some matter.' The following two synonyms also caught my attention: Disposition is defined as 'one's customary manner of emotional response, or temperament,' and temperament which is the 'manner of thinking, behaving or reacting, characteristic of a specific individual.'

All of these definitions tell me that attitude is an inner experience. In that case, I am the only one responsible for my attitude and actions which established what I say, do and think. When I deny responsibility for my thoughts, I believe what happens in my life is outside of me. When I do not take responsibility, all I can do is complain about, "how they are treating me" or "what they did to me" I will then find myself brooding about how nothing good ever happens to poor me because of the 'theys'.

I can choose to change. I can choose to pick the feelings I want to live with and change the results I desire in my life, as I take responsibility for all my thoughts, words, actions.

Each of us has free will and we choose the results we desire in our lives, we can no longer blame anyone else. That was an important aspect of reality for me to accept. It meant that in every situation I encounter, I have a choice. I believe the choices I make are directly related to how responsible I am, which is being an active participant in my evolution. I found I loved looking up words and found 'responsible' which means 'being able to make moral or rational decisions on one's own' and therefore being accountable for one's own behavior. Another definition is the ability to be trusted or to be reliable. On the other hand I can just take life as it comes which is passive. I get to choose to be active or passive in changing my life, it's up to me.

Changes In My Life

The healing continued as I began reading books Oprah shared with us for enlightenment. Some of her guests talked about a higher power, affirmations and meditating. Soon I found myself meditating a few hours a day. Oprah also taught women to take care of themselves first. I had always taken care of my children and the men in my life before myself. Wow, what a difference it made to put myself first for a change. Since I couldn't do anything else while healing, I meditated, read and jotted notes in my journal.

Journaling was not easy for me because I didn't know how to spell very well. I never found the time to go to school, study or learn how to spell, let alone understanding grammar.

THINK IT, WRITE IT

Soul Journaling

What I discovered as I tried to journal is that spelling got in my way. I could only write a few words and because I couldn't spell the words in my thoughts, I became frustrated and would stop writing. Looking at samples of people's journals, and what I called journaling were very different because my journal had a few words, some drawings, curly cues, etc. I gave myself permission to do something different and doing it my way was freedom. I started taking down words or sayings, which were popping into my head out of the blue. One day I thought I would try journaling again. To make sure I was able to capture my thoughts, I placed journals all over the house. They were available to capture any random thoughts, the positive and the negative, that had become normal conversation in my mind. As you can see, I was determined to follow through.

I would journal my thoughts and fine-tune them as needed. I'd often go back to see if they are still working for me. I discovered as I changed, so did the meaning and quality of my life as my thoughts were re-programmed. I also monitored how I reacted to my experiences and not automatically reject something just because it is different or unfamiliar. Once I had opened myself to new and different experiences, more good began to come into my life in new ways as I was building my confidence.

Some of the lessons I learned from my Soul Journaling are:

- ☐ Realize what is important in my life
- ☐ Discover my own beliefs
- ☐ Encourage myself to step out of the box
- ☐ Learn to redefine my goals
- ☐ Trust myself and my higher power
- ☐ Watch my miracles show up
- ☐ Bring the truth for my highest good
- ☐ Encourage others and praise them for taking steps to reach their goals

Affirmations

Through my journal pages, I soon realized I was writing some of the things over and over again. Affirmations were new to me or so I thought. I do remember some of the things I memorized from my Catholic upbringing, 'the Our Father, and the Hail Mary.' One day I heard myself saying, 'I am a jack of all trades and master of none.' I stopped dead in my tracks and realized the negative message I had been giving myself. I remember Oprah talking about affirmations and I realized that so many of the things I had been saying were negative. Once I realized it, I changed the statement to, 'I am a jack of all trades and master of many.' I felt I had my first affirmation that I could live by. I started collecting and writing affirmations for myself and made sure they were all positive to cancel out the negative messages I grew up with.

Looking at some of the phrases I had written in my journals, I thought I could make a deck of affirmation cards that I called "Food For Thought." I still say them often, because they help me keep my life in perspective.

Part of my healing was to pull an affirmation card and make it my job to learn it by heart. I found these cards worked miracles for me, and the key was saying them daily. I soon learned if a negative thought entered, I would reach for my "Food for Thought" cards and read them over and over until the negative thoughts passed.

As my back was healing and I was able to begin walking, I memorized my affirmations.

From Shed To Sanctuary

My Husband Ed built me a large shed in our yard when I moved in to house my lifelong belongings from storage. One day I heard Oprah say to' find a quiet space with no interruptions to be still and be with yourself'. I decided my shed would make a perfect sanctuary. My back was stronger now and I saw a big chair a neighbor threw out on the curb and I visualized myself sitting and meditating in that chair in my special space. There was no room in the shed for it so I began to clean out one box at a time to get this big beautiful chair into my sanctuary, to meditate, visualize, and write thoughts in my journal. It's all about setting your intentions of what you desire.

1998   *MIND CONTROL*

Brain Washing!

One day in the sanctuary, I was pondering how I had gotten so brain washed. Brain washed, yes! Brainwashed, isn't that where people repeatedly put words in someone's head that is not the truth? I had been lied to so often I thought it was my truth. That is when I had a light bulb moment! I knew the messages had caused me to not believe in myself. So, why can't I brain wash myself into believing I am smart, that I can do things, and to believe I am a good person? How many times do we tell ourselves that we are worthy? When do we take ten minutes for just ourselves, without guilt? I then told myself, 'What if I only write down a list of positive moments, using only positive, good words?' I now can change the words I will use, and that became one of my goals. That is how I began to develop the easy tools that you can add into your day.

Wonder Rocks

"Everywhere I am, everyone I see,
Everything I experience, I am filled with Wonder.
Life is amazing and I am a part of it."

CHAPTER 3

BACK TO SCHOOL

Editor's Note: *Stepping out of the house with a stronger back, Sheila looked for something to do and new things to learn. She looked for classes at the Adult Education Center and signed up for calligraphy and creative writing classes.*

Calligraphy

I enjoyed the calligraphy class, which helped me with my journaling and became a meditative state as I slowly learned this skill and to think about what I was writing. Each letter has to be drawn carefully so I had to concentrate! We were writing quotes from famous people and I discovered so many of them were negative. I suggested to the teacher to write more positive statements and the quotes I gave her were "let go of the past, make room for miracles," "Life is change and change is growth," and I loved how these positive statements looked in calligraphy.

One day, a classmate asked me why they should write something positive. So I asked her if she had something she wanted to change, she said smoking. I suggested that she say, "I am a non-smoker" and to keep repeating the affirmation every time she thought about smoking.

I gave her an example of using positive statements as if it already happened and how it worked for me. I hated doing dishes.

Being on my back for so long, Ed would do the dishes and it was time I changed my thinking from I hate doing dishes to "I love doing dishes."

About two weeks later Ed thanked me for doing the dishes. That was another aha moment. I learned life works, when you are teaching others to "let go of the past and make room for miracles."

By just saying the words out loud became an easy way to cause the outcome we desire. I wrote the affirmation inside of a kitchen cabinet in calligraphy. I kept repeating to myself every time I went into the kitchen, 'I love doing dishes.'

Enthusiasm Rocks

"I am alive,
aware, alert,
and enthusiastic.
My Enthusiasm Rock
radiates around me and
others near me share my
Enthusiasm."

LYING ON THE FLOOR?

Meditation

One day I noticed a meditation class across the hall from my calligraphy class. Joining the class, I learned how to develop a mantra 'I am healthy, wealthy and wise.' I found 30 minutes lying on the floor and not thinking was a very long time. The lessons and techniques learned from this class proved to be invaluable. Sometimes I would sit in front of a journal and not know where to start, so with meditation, I started receiving half sentences, which I called Mind "Stretchers" and they became a valuable tool, which allowed me to stretch my thinking.

The instructor told me she was also doing a creative writing class that night and invited me to join her.

Prayer Rocks

"I know prayer is answered,
I give thanks for what I am about to receive.
I am sending messages to GOD, my Force
my Creator, my Strength.
I know that when I pray,
I am sending to the universe my desire
for my world to be a better place,
for healing to take place, for prosperity,
for commitment, for thanksgiving, for peace.
Prayer is one of the most powerful tools I have.
Prayer plants the seed. I use prayer often.
I like talking to Spirit. I see it happens."

1997   *NO MISTAKES*

Wise Women's Circle

I went back to the Center that evening for the Creative Writing class and somehow I ended up in a Wise Women's Circle. There were candles, herbs and artifacts on a cloth in the middle of the floor. It was Halloween, and people were dressed in costumes and I sat with my writing pad. During introductions all I could say was, "Well God must have wanted me here, because I thought I was coming to a creative writing class." They all laughed, but leave it to me that the first time I leave the house by myself in years at night, I find myself in a candle-lit room with total strangers; clearly this was not a creative writing class. I had been meditating for God to lead me, and where do I find myself, in a class I may not have approached if not for a mistake. I introduced myself as a writer because I had a desire to write a book, voila'. I spoke my truth and the next morning I woke up, ran to the computer and wrote three silly stories. Never had I written anything so vivid. The process, I called was New Truth's.

I had to start somewhere with the belief I was a writer. I once heard Andy Rooney say that he would write for 15 minutes a day. That is when I began to write small booklets for my friends encouraging people to live a more positive life and enjoy the rewards. A few of the titles are:

"Don't Give Away Your Power"

"Imagination of Others"

"My Intentions"

Telling my fellow students I was a writer, when I had only written notes in my journal caused this to be my new truth. They bought it and they must have told other's when they went home, "We have a writer in the group," causing me to write again the very next day. This taught me how powerful my words can be. I have learned there are no mistakes we are always in our right place. Yes, I did eventually take a creative writing class.

I learned in the Wise Women's Circle that there are many people who believe in a higher power as I did. I heard that women were strong with equal power and must take care of themselves first. It's like being in an airplane and the oxygen masks drop, you put yours on first so you can help others. I combined the tools I learned from Oprah, and used the Circle to set my intentions of what I wanted to let go of, and what I wanted to create in my life. Stating my intentions aloud to the group as if it had already happened was very powerful.

All the techniques and tools I was learning were more energizing in a circle than being home alone. Setting intentions to do what I loved, I discovered two new passions. One passion was to work in the dirt and plant beautiful flowers. The other passion was to write a book about my passions and to discover my brilliance. Over the next years, these classes started a shift in my life.

During this time, I shared with my circles of new friends my desires and told of the miracles that happen each week. I even shared how they were happening. I never knew that I would be asked to be an inspirational speaker for the adult education 100-year celebration five years later.

WE CAN BE KIND

Boundaries

Boundaries are a very useful tool but we tend to forget how important they can be. I used to believe being unkind meant I had boundaries and others would not like or accept me. I would always say "yes" when I was asked to help with anything, I was so miserable doing stuff I didn't like doing. I was trying to be nice at my own expense. It wasn't until Oprah spoke about having boundaries that in order to be respected by others, I had to respect myself first. Agreeing to situations that caused discomfort was not respecting me. Not only did it feel uncomfortable, it would cause me to hide behind sicknesses. Being sick was an easy excuse not to do something I did not want to do, it was easier than saying no. I found myself sick in bed more and more because I allowed my mind to go there first.

As I started thinking about a universe that is created to be non-judgmental and giving, this allowed me to adjust my boundaries. I got to thinking that the universe is only giving me what I was saying. You have heard the saying, "Fake it until you make it"?

Well I believe I was faking so much sickness to get out of doing things, that I became sick all the time.

Setting my boundaries gave me the opportunity to say yes to what was fun and energizing. I was also able to release road rage and responding to unwanted phone calls until I could get into a positive state of mind.

When I became clear about my boundaries, I no longer wasted time with the 'what if's.' I defined my boundaries for myself and others respected them, the universe responded in a positive way.

Boundaries become clear to your intuition and what you focus on will show up instead. Your intentions will be so sharp that you will be able to decide faster when opportunities knock. You might think life has become easier; it is yourself respect that stands up for you. Others now know what to ask of you. If you are in the process of cleaning up your boundaries, do not get one bit discouraged by what shows up. Get excited that you are seeing it, that you have these opportunities to get another undesirable situation out of your way. Pat yourself on the back for noticing how you are honoring your boundaries. I get calls weekly from people telling me how their children are learning to set their boundaries as well. When you get use to saying no, even that starts to become normal and you do not even fret about it. Instead of fretting, you are telling yourself how proud you are of cleaning out another corner of your life. You will start to see life clearer. Life starts to see your goals, and sends tips to help as you get a clearer picture of what is important in your life. Make sure you are top priority, isn't that what you want the universe to see?

I know I would not even think to ask a friend to do something that they have already said no too. I would look for someone who enjoys doing it, and ask them. Example: I needed to find a leader for a group of children. I had three friends come to mind. The first one had turned me down before; saying the kids are difficult for her. She respected herself when sharing that information. I now respect her by not asking. The second person usually says yes to me for any reason. Then I remember that she comes up with wonderful excuses or calls at the last minute, telling me why she can't do it. The third person gets all excited when I call her. She starts telling me how this is such a grand idea and it will help her with another project as it is right inline within her goals of life.

I learned I could go through life giving my power to others or standing up for who I am today.

The Blame Game

In 1996, I decided that I would no longer blame my condition on what someone else did or did not do. No longer was I going to say, "If Peter had not done what he did, I would not have to do this." Or, "If the company had sent me a reminder, I would not have missed a payment."

I had to let go of all excuses, and stop blaming someone else for the conditions that put me where I did not like to be. I was going to get a handle on my desire to blame put elsewhere, and recognize it as shifting the responsibility away from where it belonged. In blaming, I was not likely to see the situation clearly enough to learn from it, because I would be too busy peddling blame.

This started with a friend reminding me of a big mistake I had made. I have never looked at it as an error in judgment, because I felt as though I had no other choice, that it was not my fault. She hit a nerve, a big enough one to make me sit up and listen to myself. I noticed that the first thing I did was to start explaining the circumstances of why I had to make this choice. Boy, were they good and many! I started to back track to each choice I had made. In taking this time, to reflect, I identified many area's that I could have made a different choice.

It is easier to look back when we are safely away from the situation. As I looked back, I can see I was powerful and I didn't recognize it. Yes powerful. All these years I felt I needed excuses allowing me to justify my choices. When letting others make them for me, I was giving away my power. I gave it away so I would not have to stand up for the choices I had made.

I could have stood up with my power; instead I lost my power when I gave it up to a condition, or blamed someone or something outside myself. It was much easier to fall into blaming someone else for my non-actions. In this way, I was never wrong. I believe my ego was in the way.

Let us look at it through someone else's eyes. When they hear me sending blame, it sounds like I am weak. What I did not understand was that I was sending out signals of my inability and expecting them to respect my judgments. How can another person respect me, as they listen to me lay blame on another person? What they are hearing is that I do not take responsibility for my choices. They hear me giving away my power.

They know it is not in their best interest to get involved with someone who will easily send blame to them if a situation goes wrong.

Water is always looking for a way to get out. My excuses were like water, they were not solid choices. I discovered others like having solid people around they could trust not to blame them for any situation that I find myself in.

How do you know to trust a person? Listen to them. Do you ever hear them throwing blame on another person? I heard somewhere, people tell you who they are, and you just have to listen. I did not realize what that meant for a long time. When I finally got it, I discovered I needed to take responsibility for the conditions in my life. I needed to become solid. I knew the moment I started to blame someone or something, the person listening could tell I did not take responsibility and would back off. I was pushing away valuable people, responsible people in my life. Now I hear myself, when I need to take responsibility.

Evening Exercise:

Many evenings, I take the time to reflect on where I could have taken more responsibility during a day. I compassionately remind myself, "Rome was not built in a day." I take baby steps, by telling myself, 'I deserve a "Responsibility Award." Making a point to see every little improvement in myself helps me to recognize blame before it comes out of my mouth.

These days, I can just verbally give myself a pat on the back. I continually look for the awards I deserve. Now, when I think about blaming someone, I remind myself, I do not think that way anymore. This has worked to redirect my thoughts and to stop me from verbal self-abuse. I am still recovering from giving away my power, and that it is OK. What I can say is, it is getting easier and easier to take on my own responsibilities.

When I hear someone blaming another, it is my job to know they have the power to change. By me recognizing their power, it is like opening a window for them to see through. We are all powerful and must claim it and I use it to see where I can learn. Blame throwing is a waste of energy and time and has a negative reaction toward another. We are all one, and in blaming them, we are blaming ourselves. Let go of all excuses and start right now, claim back your power.

When I need help, I look for the truth in my situation by doing some "Stretchers": Answer each one of them three times, using different answers. This allows you to tap into your own wisdom and doing this for 30-days you will see noticeable adjustments. "Stretchers" remind me that I am right where I am supposed to be in the moment.

"Stretchers":

I am powerful when I …………………..

I stand up for myself when …………………..

I make good choices when ……………………

Devote pages in your journal just for "Stretchers".

Power Rocks

"I am aware of my Power.
I am aware of Power in my universe.
My family and friends are powerful.
I use my Power for good in the world and good
returns to me in abundance."

Chapter 4

Master Gardener

Editor's Note: *While Sheshe's back was healing, her neighbor would take her to Horticulture lectures and one time the lecturer asked the group, 'what were gardens like when you were a child?' 'Where were you located?' These questions caused Sheila to really think about what she wanted and how to get people really involved in finding and creating their passion. The speaker planted a seed and Sheila thought about her childhood.*

As children, I believe we all loved to play in the dirt and make mud pies. Raising her family there was no land available for a garden so she used places inside the house wherever she lived. Sheila would visit the Rose Garden, and gardening clubs as her passion grew stronger.

What evolved from this adventure not only changed

Sheila's life but has changed the lives of many children who continue to be successful by completing high school and college, and beginning their careers. You do not always have to have a degree to have a life changing effect on a child's life.

1999   *2006 MASTER GARDENER*

Living a Passion

My life was taking off and I heard about a program that educated gardeners taught by the best instructors in the field. I told My Wise Women Circle that I wanted to be a Master Gardener. It was a sixteen-week course and I would be able to give back to the community two hundred hours helping the public with many avenues of gardening. I put my application in to become a Master Gardener through the University of California Cooperative Extension (UCCE). It was my understanding that one hundred to three hundred people would be applying and only sixty would be accepted. I was learning that anything was possible when we blow up our own balloons of possibilities and self-esteem. Even though I did not have many of the qualifications, I stayed true to believing all things were possible and I did have a group of powerful women to allow me to push forward my words of desire to be in the gardening world. Just to know someone that gardens would have been a fulfillment. After my interview and having to wait six weeks for the confirmation of acceptance, I decided to act as if I had already been accepted. Every time I went by a mirror, I would put my shoulders back and proclaim, "I have been accepted into the Master Gardener program" and I practiced feeling the success of it.

On my next visit to the Wise Women Circle, I had a plan to share with them that I had been accepted in the program. This became my New Truth, using the 'fake-it til you make-it' theory. Even though I had not received the acceptance letter, I was going to tell them I had been accepted. My intention was that my desire would be answered by believing it so. I was in the truck driving out of my driveway when my mail carrier flagged me down. We chatted and he gave me my mail that I tossed onto the passenger seat and headed to the school. As I drove, I continued to practice my words. "I have been accepted in the UCCE Master Gardener Program". When I reached the parking lot, I noticed I was early, so I picked up my mail and on top was an official letter from the University of Santa Clara Master Gardener program. My 'fake-it till I make-it' worked and I happily walked into class that night and shared my success.

Not only did I volunteer, I was asked to work in the office and I got paid. My greatest success was being given the Volunteer of the Year Award. **WOW!** Looking back, I am amazed at the abundance I was able to accumulate in my life in six short years.

Generation Connection

I was blessed to teach children about gardening at a senior center. The senior's would learn about gardening, then in turn, share what they learned with children of various schools, hence the name, Generation Connection. In the first hour, we would escort three or four children and share the names of flowers, vegetables, bugs and worms. The second hour we would interact with our group of children and get them to draw or name what they saw. Mainly for me, I saw it as an opportunity to send some positive words home with the children.

I folded a post card size stock in half. I stood it up to look like a V-tent. On the front of the card I would calligraphy the child's name. This caused them to take ownership of the card. I knew many of them would proudly display the card on their nightstands showing some good words to add into their lives. On the back of the card, in big, bold calligraphy was "YOU CAN DO IT." No matter what side showed, it was encouraging.

Inside the left half of the card I wrote boldly, 'I KNOW A LOT ABOUT GARDENS.' This would allow a loved one at home to ask them, "So you know a lot about gardens?" It would cause the child to share what they saw in the garden. On the right side of the card was the Hangman game. I created the answers from what I showed them on the garden tour and it gave me another opportunity to interact with children.

1999   *MASTER GARDENER*

Kids In The Neighborhood!

Every morning before heading to the UCCE office, I was also running my program at the local elementary school where my grandchildren attended. I desired to give first and second graders back their power before class.

My grandson would catch an early bus and my two granddaughters and I waited in the play yard for classes to begin. I would sit and journal as the kids played. The children noticed what I was doing and became interested. I felt that if the children saw me journaling, they would think it was normal. I started with eight children sitting on the cement drawing and printing their names. As the weather became colder and rainy, the school allowed me into the cafeteria where I could use several long tables and benches.

Christmas Club

I created some games that taught the children to read, write and learn to repeat back the words they would write. At first, we started out with a Christmas Tree Booklet. Each booklet was a 8x14 legal sheet of paper folded in half and holes punched so rings could go through. Rings were earned by turning in their work. I then created a front cover for each journal with a place for their name so they would get use to putting their name on everything. Each journal was filled with their booklets which were new daily lessons to be included in their journals. With the Christmas Tree booklet, they wrote down their wishes. After the holidays, I asked the children what kind of a booklet they would like next.

2000   MASTER GARDENER

Pokémon Club

Pokémon was the craze at the time, so they all wanted a Pokémon on the front cover of their journals. For the first Pokémon, we took a vote and the Pikachu Pokémon won.

Pikachu is a yellow healing Pokémon and the children were drawn to it. At the time, I had no knowledge of what a Pokémon was, so I started out with a story about Pikachu and I was quickly informed by an older boy, that Pikachu does not fly, which in my story it did. So I quickly bought a book that explained each of the over 152 Pokémon's. (The Official Pokemon Handbook by Maria S. Barbo) I had heard of the games children were playing with the cards and that was not my intention. I just needed to have something the children were attracted to in order to draw children into the class. The group continued to grow because they were in a positive atmosphere.

To be able to keep up with their daily requests for a Pokémon figure on the next booklet, I put together a request form on a clipboard so they would be able to ask for the Pokémon of their choice or what they wanted to learn, this was their first Stretcher.

Stretcher:

I desire to learn more about ....

They learned that when they filled out the form they were able to get something they really wanted. Having them learn how to politely request a booklet or new pages to add to their journals was one of my goals. For each page they completed they would receive a Pokémon sticker to add to their page. Soon they had a collection of Pokémon booklets, filled with stickers of achievements.

I noticed when the children were in the hallway and were to be quiet in the line before class they would see me and yell out my name. That was against the rules. So, I showed them sign language for "I love you". This was a joy to see when I walked the halls and a line of children with the hand jesters of "I Love You".

2000   *MASTER GARDENER*

Pokémon Lady

In my neighborhood, I was known as the Pokémon Lady and it became normal to find children at my front door for some of my newest Pokémon booklets. I would put positive affirmations in the header and footers in hopes they would ask me to read it to them. When they would return and could read it back to me, they would receive a sticker as I said "I am proud of you." I was always surprised that they would remember.

I also created affirmations for them. Some Examples:

I can find a way to get along.

I can make someone smile.

If I can't say something nice, don't say nothing at all.

I like school and school is cool.

Next, I taught them "I Am" statements to boost their self-esteem.

I Am:

I am doing my best, when I know better, I will do better.

I am doing a good job.

I am proud of myself

I am a nice friend

I am a happy and honest person.

By the time the children grew up, they have all completed high school and their dreams are coming true to go to college and live their best lives.

2000   *MASTER GARDENER*

Our Promise

Because every Pokémon had a sticker, I knew I could not hand them out without a contract with each child. I did not want to have a child's feelings hurt because they wanted a certain Pokémon sticker, which might not be available. So I created a poem for them to recite before they received their first sticker. I had them recite back to me as I read the poem. The poem inside their very first Pokémon booklet was:

"I am a happy, honest person.

I promise to be happy with myself.

I promise to be happy with any sticker I get."

As soon as they repeated the poem, they received the booklet and a random Pokémon sticker. One of the lessons they learned was to be grateful for whichever sticker they received.

I liked to encourage reading and I knew of one girl who loved to read and she would bring books and read out loud as the children journaled. I created a "I love to read" page to add to her journal. Every day she read out loud she would bring me that page and I would give her another sticker.

I began writing stories about Pokémon for the readers in the group and that encouraged kindness, giving, thankfulness, helping a friend, making someone smile and politeness. I also wrote stories using Pokémon names along with the children's name about how to get along with others.

One of the booklets was a connect-the-dot number game which when all the dots were connected in the right number order would form a picture. Anytime I would see a situation that needed more positive outcome I would create a new and different activity or write a story for them. Their reward was to read to me and get a sticker.

The children would leave the booklets for me to place in a file cabinet box that I carried daily to and from the school. I would put their booklets with their journals and file them alphabetically for them to find with ease on their next visit. In the first weeks of the Pokémon Club, I was aiming for them to write their names every time they get a new booklet so I could marry them with their journals.

I couldn't wait to go through their booklets in the evenings. Remember, I have only thirty minutes with the children in the mornings. Many days I was excited to see over forty booklets were finished and handed in and hand out about seventy stickers. This means they would have to have something to show me what they had learned. I then would place a Pokémon sticker on their page and tell them "I am Proud of you." The kids were so happy and proud of what they were achieving. The point is what they were doing didn't have to be correct, it was the effort they made and trying something new was what was most important. I desired them to feel that learning was fun and rewarding.

As I went through their booklets, I remembered my mornings as a child, if something went wrong at home; I would carry those words with me all day long. I would put myself down and found the bad feelings stuck with me throughout my day. So, when the opportunity to work with small children three mornings a week came along, I grabbed it. I desired to see if my theory to be positive and use only positive words would work on the children. They were so excited they couldn't wait to run back from a bathroom break, to learn more positive words to use while playing with others in the school yard. In my class the word 'no' was never allowed.

My challenge was to come up with creative ways of teaching without the use of any negative words and keep things positive and fun.

The principal and other teachers began to notice the benefits of positive behavior. They would often listen in to hear how positive and excited the children were. I was told it made a real difference for the children and the teachers. The important thing is that the children learned to be more positive in their classes.

Awards

Why were awards in the Pokémon club so important to me? I grew up feeling I did not deserve and waited for others to recognize my efforts. I felt that my efforts were shadows, until another human being recognized them. An actor waits for the reviews to come out, in hopes that their efforts were noticed. At school, children wait in hopes that they will receive a certificate for their accomplishments. Older students go to college to get that paper to prove they achieved something great.

I would ask a child, "What award have you earned?" Their first reaction was, "None" or "I don't know." I love this part; this was my opportunity to understand the child. I know what I saw; I desired to know what they felt. After giving them a few seconds to answer, I could sense their minds going. I know they were thinking, "Why is she asking me this?" They looked confused. First thing I noticed is that their eyes and shoulders lowered because they didn't know the answer. I had been given a golden opportunity to help them find their own beliefs about themselves. I would explain to them, that they need to start receiving awards that they felt they deserved.

With this book, I desire us to help see our own efforts and be proud of ourselves. We should grow up feeling we deserve, and we will learn how to blow up your own deflated balloons. Doing these exercises daily will start you to feel a change in your perspective. It wasn't until 1998 that I went to my thirty-fifth class reunion that I received my first awards. They were silly awards, but the feeling was there, it felt good, and changed my life and my outlook.

I put a request form on another clipboard for Awards that they felt they deserve.

"An award I deserve today is ……………….."

As soon as they told me about an Award that they felt they deserved, their shoulders would lift up and a smile would fill their face.

After that, I started a list of "I Deserve Awards" for the children to receive on a daily basis. I would create pages of small awards they could request.

Here are some of the I Deserve Awards:

I brushed my teeth today Award

The Honest Award

The Polite Award

The Kindness Award

Ask a child for the Award they deserve and you will find out what strength they are working on.

Awards work on adults too!

I was subbing for an Adult Education Class and I asked the class to name some awards they deserved. There was silence in the room. Later one of the older adult men came in to help wash the teacups and shared with me that he is stuck on that question. He said he could not come up with an award for himself. I looked into his eyes and told him that I am giving him a "Helpful Award" for helping me with the dishes. I saw the proud feeling he was getting from my words. His shoulders went back and a smile reached his heart. We are never too old or wise to receive an award.

Let us take this moment to focus on some awards that we deserve. Take a slow deep breath and allow yourself to feel how proud you are of all your actions. It is when you recognize your true value, you become mentally influential by being on familiar terms with your strengths, and it allows others to see you shine brightly.

Awards I deserve:

Today, I deserve an award for ….

I give myself an award for ….

Examples:

Today I deserve an award for using patience

Today I deserve an award for being friendly

Today I deserve an award for listening respectfully

Today I deserve an award for using money wisely

Today I deserve an award for helping around the house without being asked

Success Rocks

"I am a success.
I learn from every event in my life.
Even things that I have not understood
have made me who
I am today and that is good.
I can do more than I ever believed possible.
I am living fully and embrace the
past, present and future."

CHAPTER 5

SHIFTING ENERGY WHILE REMODELING

Editor's Note: *The following is proof positive that these tools and techniques will even work on spouses.*

1998   2002 CHANGE

The Pool Table

There was a time my husband and I were doing an addition to our small home to include a larger kitchen, living room, dining room, a full bathroom, a place for a pool table, and a Man Cave. During this time, funds ran out and the construction came to a sudden halt. My father in law who was very ill came to live with us; he needed all of our energy to monitor his health and make him comfortable. The house was no longer a priority for three years. We had bought the stove, oven and dishwasher, which sat waiting for our next move. For those three years, half of our home was 2x4 walls on a plywood floor construction site.

Learning to work with my words and energy, I knew it would work for the addition to the house. I could tell people's thoughts were, "They are never going to finish". I knew the key was to change the attitude toward our addition. I had also noticed that my husband was always depressed, especially when the topic of the addition came up. Ed would go bowling twice a week and come home depressed. I asked him why? And he would grumble, "Everyone wants to know if we have done anything to the remodel, and I have to say no." This is where I decided to meditate on the situation. Knowing that I cannot change others, but I could get them thinking about something other than our situation.

I am married to a man that loves his pizza, so I took him to a pizza house to have a talk. As we were eating, I shared with him my plan. I told him to believe in me. Just trust that I know what I am doing. I told him that I wanted to buy a pool table for our addition. Having a pool table in that room was always the plan. He let me know that we did not have the funds yet. I explained that if we believe, the money will come. Shaking his head, we went to a billiard store anyway I found the oak pool table I wanted, it matched my oak dining table and hutch. The pool table was two thousand dollars and we put it on credit.

The table was delivered and I showed the men where I wanted it. They took a second look and let me know the room was not finished. I explained, I bought the table to get the energy in the room moving in the right direction.

Now the first step was complete. I had a beautiful pool table sitting in a room with plywood floors, 2x4 walls and the guts of the attic showing. Three days later, it was Ed's bowling night and I couldn't wait for his return. As he walked in the door, I noticed he was smiling. I asked him what happened. He said, "Well, they all asked me what was happening with the remodel like normal" and he was happy to tell them, "Sheila made me buy a pool table." Now they were all thinking the room was probably completed, and started making plans to come over and play. I was proud, now I had over twenty friends thinking the addition was no longer at a standstill. Anyone that came into the room would see the table and their first thoughts would no longer be negative. Mission accomplished.

I like to look for signs to tell me I did well. The second sign was a check that came in the mail before the Visa bill came. An insurance company sent us a two thousand dollar check from a policy we knew nothing about. Build it and it will come.

The third sign we received was a light for the pool table. Ed was in a golfing tournament and won a Miller Lite cardboard box pool table light. It was a perfect light for an unfinished 2x4 studded room.

It also helped that when people would visit they asked, "What is this room going to look like?" That is when I was able to run over and say, "Here is where the sink is going and the counter will go out to here. The stove will go here, etc." Now I had others visualizing what was needed to have our dream room happen. Within two months of buying the pool table, Ed had received advice about home equity lines of credit, and before we knew it, we were hearing the hammers and saws. Six months after purchasing the pool table, our home was completed. Rack 'em!

Just by changing the attitude of our situation, caused the energies to change and expand for us.

What attitudes would you like adjusted to receive a new outcome?

Stretcher:

A new outcome I would like to see is ….

Something I did differently was ….

I desire ….

CHAPTER 6

POWER CIRCLES AND BELLS

Editor's Note: *The Power Circle and Bells were a turning point for me. I knew the majority of the people in the Circle from the Center. I chose to be vulnerable and allow myself to be comfortable being open and real.*

PATHWAY TO CHANGES

Center for Spiritual Living

One of the Master Gardener's introduced me to the Center for Spiritual Living in Willow Glen. The only reason I went was that she told me she found a church with people who thought like me, and I had to see. One Sunday I heard the minister say that the words we speak are like seeds and each seed can grow into something beautiful, or wither and die. I discovered there were many people who thought and believed as I did about being positive and were walking their talk. I took classes and shared what I had learned, and people listened.

Miracles continued happening in my life. I continued setting goals and noticed I was reaching them much sooner than I thought possible. I meditated on having a circle of adults where we could verbalize and share our truths and dreams of new beginnings in our lives. I was led to read about a women's circle in Seattle that was so successful to the point that they were no longer meeting because all the women achieved their goals and they no longer needed a group. I knew I was on the right track.

I felt I was ready to start a Power Circle with women and men. I told my classmates that I had a vision for a group to meet in my home to share the work I had done and things I had learned. I had the large pool table and Ed cut a wood board that we could use for a solid surface. I was ready and they were so excited, the 'Power Circle' was born.

Editor's Note: The emails below gave Sheshe courage and support to take a leap of faith and create a Power Circle at the Center.

2001   *ENCOURAGEMENT*

Stepping Out Of The Box

"Just chill girl: It will be a smooth ride. Besides, most of my congregates are pretty easy going. You're in my prayers. Love & Blessings, Kathy"

"You know I totally support you. Breathe, all is well. You are prepared, you are READY right now. Let go, trust and know this is what you have been waiting for. It came to you, so you know it is right. Love and hugs, BJ"

"Hi Sheila, I see you being very successful with your new class. God has chosen you to lead people to a higher place through your journaling work. All will go just beautifully and smoothly. You are experienced and your professionalism will shine through. Hugs Kisses, and much Love, Nancy O"

"Sheila you are going to be just fine. You can relax and just enjoy. You have already done the hard work and you have always been prepared to do this. Just relax and revel in the moment. I enjoyed yesterday's Power Circle. It is always a special treat for me to spend time with my friends. Hugs Tanya"

"Dear Sheila, You are a child of the Great Creator!! I SHARE THE DIVINE URGE to express life. I know we are open to the One Mind and are blessed as we allow God to work through us and fulfill our soul's desires. We walk in Our YES!! You go girl!! The desire to do and accomplish more, to be more completely happy, prosperous and well, is right. I know your evening is magnificent. God is in charge and that's the truth!!

Rev. Kathleen"

"Dear Angel, My thoughts, prayers and love are with you as you embark upon the next step of your brilliant journey. As you told me last night, "you are doing God's work, (in so many words) no sweat!" I see all finding you and all of you having an evening that is more than awesome. Easily, effortlessly and in divine love. It is perfect, whole and complete and there will be just the right number of people. I can't wait to hear about it at the Thursday night Power Circle . With all of my love, Diana"

Just Take the First Step

Dr. Martin Luther King Jr. said, *"Faith is taking the first step even when you don't see the whole staircase."*

Stepping out of the box was a lesson I was working on in my first Power Circle. The Power Circle had been going strong in my home for over a year. Our group was so successful I was asked to give another one at the Center. They gave me keys and the alarm code, for me to hold a Power Circle on Monday nights. Now this was a whole new out of the box experience. Being bipolar, this was something that could trigger my anxiety. It was my job to calm myself down and tell myself all is well. The day of my first Monday night class (Power Circle) I received the above emails from my Thursday Power Circle group, showing me their support.

One of the main reasons I created a group to come together was for us to feel heard, to pay attention and to learn to listen at a special level.

There is one thing I like you to remember: When you stay positive, there are no wrong answers, they are the right answers at the moment you answer. They become opportunities of change if this is what your intentions are. The power of the universe is to give. It does not judge, it gives to you whatever you believe is the truth for you. Learning to express one's self in a positive way, allows the universal law to bring to you what you truly desire. I use this process for three reasons:

1. Life becomes easier and things fall into place for me.
2. I end up using less energy to reach a goal.
3. It makes me feel good.

Primarily Power Circles were created for me to have the opportunity to practice staying positive with my words for two hours. It became a place to strengthen our ability to bring what is most important into our lives. I have come to believe that what you think about is what you create. With a guided group on a path to see the goodness in life, the window of vision will grow in clarity. Reaching into different levels of your soul, you will feel and see huge changes in your life.

In the Circle you will share your awareness with others, without judgments. You will discover different ideas and new visions generating a new outlook in your thinking. This is a straightforward method to enable you to realize you already have happiness in your life. For part of each day, give yourself permission to experience and own moments of happiness.

Power Circles are an opportunity to be with friends new or old, or with your family in a positive setting. The guidelines are few and quickly rewarding. Tools sharpen your listening skills and create a habit of speaking in the positive. Doing it with others, allows you to become powerful, soulful and wiser. This enlightens us to recognize how to re-adjust our focus, our intentions and how we are in control of the outcome. With these tools, on the path to see the goodness in our lives, your window of visions will grow in clarity.

In a group, we come together to create a safe environment where the negative is recognized and adjusted to create positive consequences. In the two-hour session, there is no drama, just the feeling of peace. As a listener, you are not there to understand why or where others are coming from. We were there to share each other's strengths. I had to learn to listen to my intuition, and learn not to take anything personally. When we waste time taking things personally, we could be learning from it instead which makes us our own best teacher.

I also needed a place to voice my ever-changing

opinions, ideas and self-concerns without someone trying to fix me. This allowed me an opportunity later, to reflect on some thoughts, like:

'Was I expressing enough for others to get the truth from what I said, without telling them the drama?' 'Can I re-adjust my words so that I get positive support from them?'

When I hear someone offering me advice or suggestions, it gives me a feeling that I need fixing, so we avoid giving free advice. I feel we are all at a perfect learning curve for our souls to receive growth. We are doing soul work, and the soul is always learning. We are not at a Power Circle to be counseled or to be fixed. We come to discover something about ourselves. Advice or suggestions create an unsafe place to share.

Instead, it will allow you to realize what you have been putting out into the universe. It will give you a chance to examine the seeds you are planting. Ask yourself questions like:

1. Have I been putting out misinformation?
2. Could this be why, at times I do not feel heard?

Since we cannot change others and can only change ourselves, it is a grand opportunity to bring clarity, understanding and peace into your lives.

This Power Circle was so powerful that it lasted three wonderful years. I even ended up creating a *Discover Your Brilliance Workbook* and a *How does your Garden Grow Workbook* which I sold over 600 copies, by word of mouth.

HOW THE CIRCLE WORKS

Guidelines For A Power Circle & Tools

There are no wrong answers because they are the right answers at the moment we speak them. They become opportunities of change, if this is what your intentions are. The power of the universe is to give, it does not judge, and it gives to you whatever you believe is the truth.

Why do I use this process? Because of the process, life becomes easier and things fall into place faster. I use less energy to reach my goals, and it brings clarity into reality, and makes me feel good.

We learn to adjust ever so slightly, and in doing so, the outcome becomes clearer, not only to ourselves, but to the non-judgmental law of attraction.

Tools For A Power Circle, And Creating A Group

A positive outlook

A space for people to gather in one space

Invite a few friends/family members

Deck of Food for Thought Cards

Deck of Stretcher Cards

Deck of Power Word Cards

Opening/closing poems

Worksheet(s)

Bell(s)

Sharing Wand (lavender stalks or a talking stick)

Small hand mirror

Pens/pencils

Candles (opp)

HOW IT WORKS

My Process

The morning of the Power Circle I would work on materials I thought would be valuable. Looking through the materials my intuition would tell me what to work on for that evening. It is my belief that we are not broken, so nothing needed to be corrected. What I wanted was a safe space to voice ever-changing opinions, ideas and desires. We were coming together to discover what was possible for ourselves without interruptions, suggestions or counseling.

We gathered around the pool table and I would begin with opening thoughts or poems as everyone closed their eyes and began to relax. It puts us all into a mindset to allow for growth and reminded us that we can let go and think bigger. We would check in by using the Sharing Wand to talk for three minutes about our week. The rules of the house were not to try to change anyone else; we could only work on ourselves. We used colored pens and paper to doodle words of wisdom that we were hearing in the circle. I felt it opened the right side of the mind and allowed us to color outside the lines. While, we doodled, we would share our achievements and most positive moments of the week. We voted for a three-minute time limit per person. I noticed one or two people would talk, and talk, and talk, sometimes up to 20 minutes. I tried using a 3-minute timer, to watch the sands of time drift through the glass cylinder to stop them. When that didn't work as I had hoped, I thought of ringing a bell. I decided to give everyone a bell so I wouldn't look like the bad guy. We rang the bell when the timer ran out and by the fifth week, we also rang the bell every time we heard a negative word. We had such fun as we became aware of what we were really saying. We were becoming aware of the messages we were putting out into the Universe and the seeds we were sowing.

Then we used the game called ""Stretchers"." "Stretchers" are half sentences that we complete allowing us to learn about ourselves in a very positive way.

NOTE: If you are willing to do these basic "Stretchers" daily, you will see miracles showing up. Your attitude will change to move you to a wonderful state of possibilities. This game allowed us to stretch our thinking to include what we really desired in our lives and to move out of what no longer served us.

Here are a few examples of "Stretchers" we would write and discuss:

This week I was proud of myself for: ……

I recognized answered prayer when: ……..

I always feel good after: ………

Editor's Note: I have participated in the Power Circles over a three-year period and the Power Words was one of the best ways to be creative as we saw ourselves in a new way.

9-17-1993   *LESSONS FROM LIFE*

Power Words

After the "Stretchers" are completed, each person would pull three cards from the "Power Word" deck and create a sentence using the words, which became a personal affirmation. Many times, we would hear other people's three-word affirmation and would busily jot it on our doodle page to remember.

An example of six power words are:

Determined, positive, desire, purpose, growth, wisdom

Using three of the six words, create an affirmation, which could be:

"I desire positive actions in my new growth."

Miracles Rocks

"*WOW! Miracles are happening every day in my life.
I expect an abundance of miracles and am ready,
willing, and able to accept
miracles to occur on a regular basis.
Miracles change my life.
I choose to see the miracles of life daily.*"

Mirroring

Near the end of Power Circle, I had a mirror that each person would hold and take turns mirroring back, in the most positive way, what they heard by using positive words. We would go around the circle passing the mirror from person to person. The person, holding the mirror would share whatever they wanted about the session, and not be interrupted by anyone else. When they finished the mirror would pass to the next person and so on. An example might be that one person had a challenge with an older person in their family. They would explain briefly, what happened and what they did to help the person. When we mirrored back, we would pass a small hand mirror. This let us know that the person is mirroring back something she heard, like, "I heard you were understanding, patient and resolved the issues within your family."

My personal experience with the mirror when we first began was that the mirroring did not always reflect back what I was trying to say, and because of that, I noticed I felt misunderstood. This is what I would call 'a red flag' and when this happens, it is a gift, embrace it. It will help you realize what you have been putting out to the universe without knowing it. It gives you a chance to examine the seeds you have been planting. If you sometimes feel misunderstood, ask yourself questions, like: 'Am I clear in my communication?' 'Could this be why, at times I do not feel heard?' Since we cannot change others and can only change ourselves, it is a grand opportunity to bring clarity to ourselves through this activity.

Understanding this process is still most helpful today. I found it was a gift to realize the way I expressed my own words sometimes caused me to be misunderstood. This is an opportunity to take the time to share with the group again using new words and hear it mirrored back in the way I intended. Remember, the listeners are going to mirror back the way they intuitively hear you. There will even be times as one is mirroring back, an answer someone else needed shows up. This is what can happen when we are open to change and possibilities. We can never take 'mirroring' personally, it is a tool and it becomes a gift not only to you, but also for the listeners. Knowing this and understanding the process could be adjusted, gave me peace of mind. I realized I could not expect the universe to co-create with me if I could not explain it to myself. That is why it is so important

NOT to be questioned or interrupted when sharing. Very often people will find their own answers as they speak without other people's opinions. All we have to do is listen, and give back positive feedback of good qualities with the mirroring technique.

I became so inspired with the Power Circles as I noticed how people were making positive changes in their lives, I began making more games which will be shown later in my website.

I gave Power Circles in local churches and anywhere someone would ask and still to this day I continue to give them when requested. Being at home, I found forums on the internet where I could hold online Power Circles. IMVU (Instant Messaging Virtual Universe) is where I started my first internet Power Circles and now I hold one on Facebook, where hundreds come in from all over the US, as well as Australia, India, and Canada, share and do daily "Stretchers". People get lessons and interact positively to reach their individual goals.

Power Circles were created for a home based group with an opportunity for personal empowerment. It is a gathering of family and friends to expand in positive growth. Coming together encourages self-awareness, and self-discovery through power listening. The Circle is a safe place to allow people's brilliance to shine. Focus becomes sharper as one begins to see things differently. As people witness positive changes taking place in their lives, each is encouraged to try something else new.

I even do mini Power Circles on the phone and whenever someone comes to visit. We go through the affirmations and then draw five of the stretcher cards and we both answer them. In the writing and editing this book, my editor and I would begin the session with a hug, "Stretchers" and affirmations.

I was amazed at how effective it was to shift the focus to look for the good and then watch good show up. I learned to notice when I was running old tapes that no longer served me and realized that I could change the tape and get exactly what I wanted. No longer a victim of circumstance, I was able to manifest my heart's desire simply by knowing all things are possible and therefore why not for me too. I've come to realize that there is an abundance of good and that good is available to all who believe it's possible.

Growth Rocks

"The power and glory of growth.
All living being grow and evolve.
Growth never stops.
As long as I breathe, I am changing.
My body is renew itself,
my mind is ever absorbing new things,
The world is experiencing new
awareness's through my growth."

Editor's Note: Sheila has two natural children and three others who came into her life and call her Mom. There are several grandchildren and friends and their children have adopted her as Mom, Grandma Sheshe, or Auntie Sheshe. Children from the neighborhood and everywhere she goes gravitate to her like she is the pied piper.

2001   *BLESS THE CHILDREN*

GOD Always Brings Us Our Children

My belief growing up was that God always brings us our children. When I was 19, I had my daughter and son and told I would never have any more children; it was too dangerous and would tear a hole in my womb. I still knew God would bring me my children. After an eight-year marriage, I walked away from the marriage with four children, two that I gave birth to, the second against the doctors' orders, and two girls that needed a Mom and some love. Years later, I remarried an old flame and I received another Daughter Billie Jo. The marriage failed and in time, she came to live with me. God brings us the children who need our touch or who are here to touch us.

Tranquility Rocks

"I am serene. I am at peace.
The beauty of my world surrounds me.
I create tranquility in my being.
I listen for the sounds of a butterfly.
My spirit soars. My life is amazing."

How the tools worked for my daughter and an on-line friend

My Daughter Billie Jo grew into a fine woman, called me one day, and said she was ready for a divorce. It wasn't like the other years when she talked about leaving the marriage when I knew they were just getting to know each other. In the twelve years of their marriage, they had two boys, and my son-in-law wanted to save the marriage. They had already discussed that she was taking the younger Autistic child. The oldest son would remain with Dad. Keep in mind, these are two beautiful people who were just not on the same page.

I figured it was time to go visit and see if the marriage could be saved. Ed and I flew from California to Florida as soon as possible. Billie Jo and my son-in-law were willing to give my tools a chance. For two weeks before we flew to Florida, my daughter was doing the lessons in my on-line Power Circle group. My son-in-law was to send me daily emails with twelve things for which, he was grateful.

We spent a week with them to see if they both could come to terms with whatever was going to happen. Of course, I did not want them staying together if they were going to be unhappy. Moms always want their children to be happy so, I convinced them to hold off separating until we got to Florida. We stayed a week at a nearby hotel, where they picked us up daily and we spent eight or more hours with them and my grandsons. We did small exercises that I do in a Power Circle, and we rang the bell when we heard any negative remarks. I shared with them affirmations I felt would cause some breakthroughs. Mostly I pointed out the good things I saw them doing with each other, and how special they are.

One night, Billie Jo and I took a long walk so she could vent which allowed her to let me know where she was coming from. This was the only time I wanted to hear the dramas. At the same time she knew I would be giving her "Stretchers" when she needed to open her thinking a little further. I was looking for her real passion and I continually directed her to keep that in the forefront in her mind. My questions to her were, 'what do you really want to be doing'? or, 'do you really want to leave?' It is in the unspoken words, you can sometimes acquire clarity. I was looking for what she desired in marriage. Was it respect she was looking for or trying to find out where they were not connecting?

Now remember I had been receiving my son-in-law's twelve gratitude's daily for over two weeks. She had no idea the beautiful words he had shared with me. As I read his emails, I could feel his growth shifting, and I could see where he was starting to connect to the families dynamic. I could see and hear him getting it. So what I told her on our walk was to let go of the 'thought' of leaving, at least while we were visiting. Just let a window of opportunity shine in on the marriage. I reminded her of the mustard seed, and I desired for her to have that much faith that their marriage could heal and bloom. I suggested leaving the opportunity open that they could come together and both be at peace and love what each is doing every day as a family. I also told her that the lesson she was having with him, was going to follow her into the next relationship and wouldn't it be better if she worked it out with him first? So, she said she would do her best to keep an open mind.

Two weeks after we returned to California, I heard from Billie Jo. She let me know that they fell in love again. They started doing their gratitude's together, use daily affirmations as a family, and continued using the bells, even with the boys. It has been several years now, and they feel as if they are soul mates and on the same page. A year later, they renewed their vows on a beach as a family. I am blessed.

I believe you will get a good understanding of what you will receive by reading testimonials from Power Circle participants later in the book.

WELCOME TO MY HOME

Knight in Shining Armor –
Diane Witherington

I met this sweet kind lady on a trip and heard her story. What I saw was a very giving person with no boundaries. Diane would give the shirt off her back, if someone needed it. Her self-esteem balloons were deflated, on the floor, and being stomped on. With low self-esteem and no boundaries, she found herself out of her twenty-two year marriage. Her husband was one of the civic leaders of their town. She now was without her beautiful big home and her husband took her car and gave it to their son. She was staying with her daughter and son-in-law, until she could find a place of her own. Her only income was a small social security check. Being a wife, mother, grandmother and a stay at home mom, was the only thing she knew. I felt that if she completed my course of Sheshe Miracles she could have anything she desired.

She flew here for two weeks, ending up staying five in the guest room. I shared with her the tools that you find in *Discovering Your True Brilliance.* We used the 'delete bell' daily with each other if we found ourselves going toward the negative. The bell always reminded us to stay in the positive. We did "Stretchers" three times a day, in this way she would learn to blow up her own balloons. She also took the time to journal nightly in one of my online Power Circles.

As she started to like herself, she became happier. One night we were sitting under the stars and visualizing her desires. I asked her what her goals were for her future. We went into all the normal things like her passions and desires. Then I asked her "What is it you really want if all things were possible?" She named off a bunch of typical desires and I told her to go for the gusto, God will bring you anything. "If all things were possible, what is it you really desire to happen when you leave here?" I believe we were in our fourth week and she laughed and told me, "I desire a Knight in Shining Armor on a white horse." "Ok," I said, "What does that Knight in Shining Armor look like to you?" She told me, "Someone that loves her southern cooking, is a good provider, a romantic, and loves dogs. Must also have a hot tub" and we laughed.

After she went home, she met a man on the internet. Not only did he live eight miles away, but also had dogs and a hot tub. He is charming, wonderful, successful and a southern gentleman. She had left my home in the summer and was married by Christmas. It has been over four years and they are still romantically married. She got her Knight in Shining Armor!

Chapter 7

Forgive And Let Go

Editor's Note: *As we move through life we learn that we can no longer carry the pain and hurts from the past. As hard as it is to believe, whatever happened helped us become who we are today. The lesson of forgiveness is not for the other people, it is for us to take the higher road so that we can move to Discovering Your True Brilliance.*

2001   *BREATHE AND RELEASE*

Forgiveness

I have learned that anyone who cannot take no for an answer is only trying to control me. I love this saying, because saying no was a challenge for me. The reason I could not say no to anyone is that they would not take no as the answer. Having to say no to someone was hard enough the first time, let alone a second time. I needed friends that took no for an answer and respected my decisions. How could I learn what I liked doing, if I was never allowed to make a choice.

Knowing I was not being true to myself was a struggle. I didn't have the muscle to exercise the power of choice or to turn away from people who would try to control me.

It was in my best interest to learn to see others differently. I love the saying, "People come into our lives for a reason, a season, or a lifetime."

I was a person who loved to help others. I thought, if I could show my husbands how to live, and how they could be happy we could be happy together. Of course, they had their own ideas.

In early 1990, I decided I needed to change my perspectives. For twenty-five years I held on to the old ways and I then had to face it, the old way was not working. I needed to change; I needed to get my power back; I needed to forgive. I was getting angry at life, and becoming like my husbands with my attitude. It seemed I was fighting with myself. I had read over and over again, in changing yourself, others will change around you. At the time, that did not make a bit of sense. But what about the person I was running away from? If mother was right, I still had to deal with that situation. I reminded myself that I was a forgiving person and could forgive those trying to control me. Forgiveness does not mean having dinner with them; it is for the purpose of healing our insides.

During the forgiveness process, I came to understand that the bad decisions I had made and the people involved needed forgiveness for my own well-being. If I could forgive them I would also be forgiving myself and it was important that I took care of myself, or maybe I needed them in my life to learn how to forgive. When I felt the pressure of unforgiveness at the top of my chest, I would think peace and breathe instead. It is like the marshmallow on a stick. I remember the first time I stuck a marshmallow into the flames and it caught fire. As I learned to have patience with flame and fire, I came into control. My feelings are like those marshmallows. Soon people from my past did not cause the flames to flare up and blister my chest. The healing had begun; forgiveness was the key. As the days wore on, every time I felt my chest flare up I told myself I was not going to feed their power. I would reflect on peace and happier times. Sometimes I would only feel the peace for a few seconds; in time, the seconds became minutes. I had to start being true to myself first and say No without guilt while taking responsibility for my own actions. As I take a break throughout my day, I take a deep breath and I inhale sweet thoughts of joy. I am charging up my batteries with courage, love and strength. I am full of hope, knowing all the good thoughts I have focused on will always multiply.

Exercise: Sit back and focus on the good of last week. Let us remember the tiniest good things that came our way. Look at the wisdom we used, the wisdom to which we are proud of ourselves for imagining. We are proud of ourselves for forgiving, not running away, and for standing up to the lion and watch the lion disappear. Be proud of looking at life full on, and accepting all its good.

Complete these "Stretchers" to gather your pride, strength, wisdom, courage and self-love:

I used wisdom this week when I ....

I used courage this week when ....

I saw good in my week when ....

Continual use of this exercise allows your vision to become stronger faster. I figured it tweaked me to the point I was no longer attracting men that needed fixing or people trying to control me. Wow, this process worked much faster than I expected. The shift in my thinking brought immediate change. At the end of 1990, I met my now wonderful husband of twenty some years. It worked!

Joy Rocks

"Joy makes me tingle.

When you look at your Joy Rock,

remember a moment of great joy in your life.

Experience it again and again.

You can never have too much joy in your life.

I rejoice in Joy.

Open your life to Joy."

Editor's Note*: Everything we say can be an affirmation. Affirmations can help the healing process or prolong it for a very long time. An affirmation is a statement that something is true. One of my favorite affirmations is, "All Is Well." When I can make that statement throughout the day, I feel lightness within me. Another affirmation I use often is, 'this is the best day of my life."*

1998   I DECLARE

Favorite Affirmations

My favorite affirmation as I was going through life's trials and tribulations was, 'this too shall pass,' and 'everything is working out for the highest good for everyone concerned.'

The following affirmations I find useful to keep me on moral ground. If something rears its head, I find a moment to run the affirmations through my thoughts; this is another tool of setting my boundaries. One or more would bring me comfort or a light bulb moment. When you have a friend going through something, take them through these affirmations and they will have a light bulb moment as well.

Affirmations:

I can't change others, I can only change myself

Anyone who cannot take no for an answer is only trying to control me

Time is on my Side

I deserve inner peace and I accept it now

I expect the best and I will get it

Look with wonder at that which is before me

My healing is already in progress

Today is a day of completion

As you think, so shall it be

As one door shuts, many more open

You think it; you create it

I am doing my best, and when I know better, I will do better

I am fully equipped for the divine plan of my life

I am filled with energy and enthusiasm

I deserve all that God desires for me

I am powerful, I am unlimited

I am always safe and divinely protected

It is none of my business what other people think of me

My spiritual healing is already in progress somewhere in inside of me.

If one of the affirmations makes you question, take the time to get to know it. I have found affirmations can transform your thinking. What you get out of it when first reading it, and what you get out of it by saying it 5 to 10 times a day, can bring you some wonderful Ah-ha moments.

Part 3

Chapter 8

Stories Of How These Tools Work In My Life

Editor's Note: *Following are a few stories Sheshe would like to share of how positive thinking, changed the way she moved through life to make better decisions and continues to work for her today.*

1995   *EMPOWERMENT*

Controlling Our Reactions

In 1995, I remember having erased the hard-drive on my first new computer, just by pushing the wrong buttons. I flew into the living room, where my husband to be, was watching TV. I was so angry at myself and raging as I was trying to tell him what happened. He yelled, "Stop! This is not how you handle this situation!" I stopped in my tracks. My panic and tears stopped. I was confused. His words hit home, I had never thought there could be another way to handle a catastrophe. I became more open to my choices in the way I should handle my reactions to a situation. Let go of the past; make room for miracles. Having a moment to redirect my thoughts, will in time, bring about new results. I learned to recognize the signs of negative self-talk and to become more constructive. I became aware of how I expressed small failures, especially in the presence of a child. This is a course of thinking that unlocks your true given power.

The people around us who are our role models teach us self-judgment. As small children, we automatically look up to anyone bigger than us. We watch how that person handles their challenges. My mother handled everything as a huge catastrophe, with drama, crying, self-belittling, and then complete anger. Putting the wrong ingredients into a recipe caused her to express anger out loud. Did she forgive herself and find a better way to handle things? Did she handle it with ease and calmness? The way in which things are handled, shows a child the way they are supposed to react.

2001 PAIN, BLISTERS – OUCH!

Human Band-Aid

Making major changes in my life, there were times when I would worry. The first signs were the fever blisters on my lips I know this because I would tell myself, "See I have proof." Pains would show up in different ways. I would have a good excuse to go to bed and feel sorry for myself and not deal with life that day. The pain gave me an excuse for my own pity party.

One day I recognized fever blisters, aches or pains were my "Red Flags." I decided to take responsibility because things were showing up when I no longer desired them. They had become an annoyance. Some had become too normal for noticing. I finally told myself "Dis-Ease" is no longer going to control my way of life. I am ready to take responsibility for my actions. I will decide if and when, I need a day off; no longer will I need an excuse; so I gave myself permission for a day off without pain, guilt or shame. My affirmations were, "My body is powerful, it can heal itself" and "This day I am sending all aches and pains away." I also accepted that my powerful imagination had become so real that I could take charge of my life. I was ready for a new and exciting day of completion, fun or rest. That has become my Human Band-Aid.

When I am aware of a pain starting, I reflect on the obstruction I am feeling. I affirm, "I have time for me." I would forgive myself for ever doubting my wisdom and I sat somewhere comfortable to meditate. I allowed myself to focus totally on me. I find lighting a candle causes me to stay in focus. I sometimes want quiet music in the background, using anything that will remind me to just be. I then started looking at each thought roaming around in my head. After seeing that nothing is really worth concern, I saw the images that did not benefit me and I gave them permission to leave. I would tell my inner child, all is O.K., allowing it to know I am now in control. Reminding my inner child that all is safe, I am safe; I have handled harder situations. I repeat to myself that I am living in perfect health. If I need to, I will run through some of the things I have accomplished.

By reflecting on my accomplishments, I start to see how purposeful I really am. Reflecting back shows me when I have put my whole effort and belief in myself. There has never been anything that I have not truly succeeded doing. I re-examine, "Do I have a heart in what I am doing?" or "How can I do this from my heart?"

I remind myself, I am here now, living in the present. I now give myself permission to let go of stuff that is not required, un-cluttering my mind. This allows me to concentrate on my priorities. If I feel a challenge, I will ask myself, what is essential to have accomplished and is there a time limit? When I can answer the questions, I meditate on my top three priorities. I remind myself to write down my purpose without beating myself up. This permits me to know if I am side tracked or if I am enriching my goals. I am now allowing myself to nourish my strengths instead of what I thought were weaknesses. As I find myself in profound awareness with respect to my abilities, I notice I am no longer feeding or embellishing the pain.

I call this my "Human Band-Aid" method. Someday, I will not need a human Band-Aid; until then, it still comes in so very handy. Just using the Band-Aids, means all things are possible. I have been telling everyone and myself that I believe this self-talk works. I can add this day to my growing list of miracles. Every time I think about this wonderful breakthrough, I reassure my inner child, all is O.K. I remind myself that the old ways of handling the pressures of life, using pain to give permission to feel will no longer work.

Here are some affirmations (Human Band-Aids) you can use:

I am in control of my life.

I trust my decisions; knowing I am making them with love for myself and others.

Open me up, turn me on, use me, all is well.

Everything is working out for the highest good for everyone concerned.

I am filled with energy and enthusiasm.

When affirmations do not hurt others, or me they are coming from my higher self. That to me is God in action, and that is good. I can enjoy the rest of my day and embrace my life with true meaning. My days without pain have become a gift, and my life is the greatest gift realizing the world is a wonderful place to be. I recognize the pain was just a red flag. Now I can be accountable for my days using this and other tools. I now have clarity and I give myself a pat on the back for being aware. I envision myself in perfect health and wellbeing. My body is healing as I complete these affirmations:

I let go of…………………………..

I am blessed when …………………………

I am grateful when ....

I have accomplished ....

My red flag was ....

I know my body is healing when ....

9-2002   *ENJOY THE EXPERIENCE*

DMV

I like to give myself lessons while I go through things in life. I went to the Department of Motor Vehicles and decided it would be a great place to practice the "no blame" exercise. I would create just what I wanted in my mind and not blame any situation or person for my experience. In the past, I rarely came without a lot of drama and poor me stories. This time, I was going there with a positive attitude, no matter what happened. No excuses, no blaming others.

The morning started out with a bad hair day. I threw a hat on, shoved the hair inside of it and told myself not even a bad hair day was going to stop me. I remembered as I was driving, I should have made an appointment, and I would just take my chances, nothing was going to detour me from my mission. I was ready to take my power in hand.

Entering the building, I was told by a man at the door, "You should have made an appointment?" Without taking away his power, and telling him that I knew, I smiled and asked, "Could there be a way to get around it?" He, while owning his power, pointed and suggested that I stand in that long line over there. I thanked him for his kindness. By making him feel good, I knew he would be rooting for me inside. When I had first walked in, my imagination could have seen him as uncaring, but my higher self would not permit that after setting my intention. It turned out, every time I walked in front of his desk, to go to another line he would wink or give me a thumbs up. I had created a friend for the day. There is always power in two.

In the long lines, I decided others needed to receive some of my cheerfulness. I smiled at everyone. I started to give up a couple times, but instead, I closed my eyes for a moment and brought God into our line. I sent good feeling to everyone, especially the workers behind the counter. Soon workers felt the good feelings and opened up two more windows. Before I knew it, I was visiting with someone in line. Several people asked me what I was in line for, I would say, "A miracle." Now I knew those words were going around in their heads, if only in jest. I am sure it was better than what they had been thinking.

Now as I am walking up to the widow, repeating in my head, "Every person is a golden link into the chain of my good." The answer was always Yes. The lady at the window spoke sharply to me. I could tell she needed someone positive. People must have been stealing her power all morning and I recognized that it was my job to let her feel her power again. With the biggest smile I could muster up, I said, "I have a challenge, and I know you will be the right person to help me solve it. You look like someone who can create miracles." She softened right before my eyes. I had squarely put the responsibility on myself, and not on her, as I heard others in front of me do. At the end of her day she needed to go home feeling as though she had helped people. Kindly, she explained to me what papers I was missing. She told me she felt bad that the rules were the way they were. I told her, "I knew I came to the right person." As I started to leave, she whispered to me, "You could do this by mail." She also gave me some new paperwork and I left her window feeling one-step closer to a great result. I told the person in line behind me, "This lady is very wise, you are lucky to get her window."

One down and one to go I told myself as I stopped by my gentleman friend at the door. I thanked him again and asked if I could again get in a line without an appointment for renewal of driver's license? He said with a wink, "with your luck, you can get into the line over there, it just opened."

I walked over to the shortest line in the building. I was thanking God and all those around me for this short line. Things were going smoothly. Again, I greeted this woman in the same fashion as the last. When she had taken care of her part, she sent me over to the line in front of the camera. This was not expected. "Not to worry," I told myself. I reminded myself to continue to stay positive and happy inside, allowing this to be what the camera was going to pick up.

Standing in front of the camera, wearing my hat with my long hair shoved inside, the man tells me to take off my glasses. I immediately remembered that I hated pictures without my glasses, "Stop," I scolded myself: I sure did not need to go there. I said to myself instead, I am going to take a great picture with good attitude.

Next the man was asking me to do something; I needed to ask him what it was because I was not listening. He was telling me to take off my hat. I laughed, and asked him if he was joking. "No" was his straightforward response and I could only laugh as I took off my hat. God could be funny too. I was surprised to notice, no anger or any of the old emotions were arriving. I stood in front of the camera believing my inner beauty better show up. To this day, I believe that my driver's license pictures are the best I have ever taken. Now whenever a camera shows up in front of me, I remind myself to allow my true self to show up and I take responsibility for my attitude. I let Spirit shine forth as I get out of the way.

Editor's Note: Money is a medium of exchange; it is energy and useful in our society. People would rather talk about their sex life than talk about their money.

2002   GOLD, SILVER, BILLS, COINS

Money

While sorting and cleaning my home, I heard myself say, "I wasted money on this item." "I do not have enough money." I realized I said it so often that it showed up in my thinking enough to cause me to feel bad about myself in the way I chose to spend money. It is like a thought that has been in my thinking for so long, that I don't pay attention to it.

I asked myself, "Could this notion be in the way of my growth?" "Is this my next lesson to improve my thinking and my self-worth?" Yes, and I decided to take the bait believing it will make tremendous growth within me. Affirmations are replacement thoughts or 'new truths,' so I took the time to find a more productive way to talk about money using these affirmations:

"I make good choices with my money"

"I spend money with wisdom"

My income is increasing daily.

Unexpected money is coming my way.

Using these statements could improve one's life. Therefore, I decided to let go of the un-truth that I waste money, and recognize the reality. I chose to stop the mixed messages that did not serve me nor give me abundance. It is a gift to recognize our un-useful messages as we become aware of our thoughts and recognize the consequences.

Activity:

List different ways you tell yourself that you use money wisely. Answer these "Stretchers" to clear your thinking:

I am willing to use money ....

Money shows up when ....

I use money wisely when I ....

My friends use money wisely when they ....

Another activity was to prepare a page in my journal for recording times when I was proud of the way I used money wisely. By reading your choices allows you to recognize how you may have been using money wisely all along. Ask your friends how they feel they use money wisely. People would rather talk about their sex life than talk about their money.

CHAPTER 9

TESTIMONIALS FROM POWER CIRCLES

Editor's Note: *I believe you can get a good understanding of what you will receive by reading the testimonials from Power Circle participants.*

Nancy Garrison

"I was amazed at how effective it was to shift my focus to looking for the good and then seeing good show up. I learned to notice when I was running tapes that weren't what I really wanted and realized that I could change the tape and get exactly what I wanted. No longer a victim of circumstance, I was able to manifest my heart's desire simply by knowing all things are possible and therefore why not me too. I've come to realize that there is an abundance of good and that good is available to all who believe it's possible.

Sheila's coaching and real life exercises through Power Circles has taught me to use only words that express my highest and best good. There is no room for resentment by only wishing the best for every human being. When one is doing well, we all do well as we are all connected. I have been coached by one who has proven it works by practicing what she teaches. I now know that every situation can be transformed into good by choosing to see it as being so. Thanks Sheila!"

Love, Peace and Tranquility." Dr. Jim Chou

"In this world today when people are always stressed out and complaining, it's refreshing to bring out only the positive. There are more than enough negatives out there and it is too depressing. We all need positive vibrations and testimonials. If it can be done and you believe in it whole heartily, then it will be done. Sheila's positive feelings truly do bring out the very best in everyone. Each of us who practices the positive journalizing will soon see an amazing transformation and it will make a difference in everyone you touch. This is so essential for everyone especially family and loved ones, whom we all often take for granted. Sheila's persistence in sharing her thoughts, love and good will make an impact on all those who listen and follow through. Wonderful things are bound to happen because you wanted and willed it and all the answers are out there for you to create and make it happen. Positive and good thoughts and deeds cannot fail because it's in tune with the universe! Best of luck in all your endeavors to you Sheila."

Toni Costa

"This work has a ripple effect that touches all areas of my life long after the work is completed. It awakened my creativity and caused it to flow. This is powerful. Participating in a Power Circle caused me to truly feel heard."

Joanne Rosso

"After one month in your Power Circle, it plunged

me deeper in synchronicity and compassion than I have ever imagined possible. Your mirroring technique, "active listening" has changed my life. I now choose my words with care, leaving no doubt in my communication and experience a greater satisfaction".

Tish Foley

"Since taking the class, I feel more empowered by changing many belief patterns and living life in faith, confidence and abundance. My sister and I took the class together which brought us to a deeper spiritual connection. Life is filled with miracles. Thank you Sheila for being an inspiration!"

Gail Griffith

"I was extremely anxious the night I attended a Power Circle group for the first time. I shared my dilemma, pain and frustration as well as steps I was taking to help heal the situation. I'll never forget the outpouring of love and support as the group validated me in ways I'd not considered possible. Sheila sketched a rose on a large sheet (flip chart) and filled it with traits and actions the group observed about me. It's still on my wall as a reminder of who I am and the women who helped me know the truth. In Gratitude,"

Sandra Todd

"I found I learned to express myself in a positive way and thereby opened myself to more positive people, thoughts and experiences. I felt less burdened, "lighter", supported, able to have more fun, put things in perspective, feeling more in control. I now look for positive things to say instead of trying to fix it."

Diana Witherington

"I have been using Sheshe's online site and doing one on one Power Circles with her for a few months now. I was first drawn to Sheshe by her magnetic sunny personality. As I came to know her better, and what she is all about, it blew me away. Sheshe understands the fundamentals and how to apply them to live a happy abundant life, and has created the tools to get people going in that direction. To see what she and people who have used her tools have overcome in their lives is an inspiration and a testament that you don't have to be held down by circumstances, you have the power to be what you want to be. Thanks Sheshe."

Deborah McDermott

"I learned today and yesterday and the day before that this group is awesome and so is everyone in it!!! I have a friend who was diagnosed with cancer and

I told her about Sheshe and everyone in her group and how powerful positive thought is. I come back to the group often to remind myself and everyone that Positive stays with you if you let it. Thank you Sheshe once again for letting me help one more person with your wisdom."

B. J. King – Editor

I met Sheila at the Center for Spiritual Living and instantly felt there was chemistry. I attended her Power Circles for a couple of years and always left uplifted. When she asked me to edit her book, I was delighted to do whatever I could to help her. We have been working together for about three months and every time we meet it is like a breath of fresh air for me. We always begin with setting our intentions, prayer, "Stretchers", Power Words and Food For Thought Games.

About a week or so, she asked me to listen to something she found to be included in the book. We were so close to the end, I didn't want to add anything new but I listened. I was amazed at the description she read of how the group was defined, and what kept this person coming back. When she finished she uncovered the name and it was mine written August 29, 2002.

This is how I defined the group: "Energetic, smart group of women who help each other see the best in themselves and who allows each person to hear what they say."

What keeps me coming back? The energy and growth I continue to experience and the laughter plus the total acceptance by all encourages me to set goals and be accountable.

Smile Rocks

"As you smile at the Rock, it will
make you laugh inside
at the same time. Smiling always feels good.
So take good care of your Smile Rock
and it will smile back.
Smiling makes my spirit soar.
Smiles stay deep in my heart."

CHAPTER 10

GAMES

Editor's Note: *These games are an easy way to shift my moods and attitudes as I help others do the same. I find that I use them more and more with my clients and in my PlayShops. I have shared some of the games with several people and they already see changes in their lives. They feel very blessed to have something so easy and empowering to use on a daily basis.*

Basic Stretcher Game

If all you do is these basic "Stretchers" daily, you will see miracles begin to unfold sooner than you think possible. Using these tools is a fun, and enjoyable way to recognize and see how special and powerful you really are, and how to bring forth new awareness that you may not have thought you had. Avoid repeating an answer, unless it is said in a different way and it is positive.

Sometimes I would sit in front of a journal and not know where to start, so with meditation, I started receiving half sentences, which I call Basic "Stretchers" and they became a valuable tool.

I started with these Basic "Stretchers":

I am grateful for ………………………..

I am blessed when……………………...

I felt loved when …………………...

I desire ………………………...

I am willing to let go of …………………

Basic Mind "Stretchers", lead to stretching the ability to recognize the tiniest miracles. They bring forth opportunities for enjoyment and daily awareness. They allow you to see what you have been learning throughout each day. Not only does it stretch the imagination, it stretches your viewpoint, causing growth. They take you into the back door of your thinking because back door thinking moves you out of your ordinary thoughts. It is a way of putting together words you would never have taken the time to reflect on. It is with these feelings of positive thinking that allows you to live each day to the fullest and to receive a restful sleep. Every day you wake up, rejoice, and remind yourself, today is a new day with the opportunity to start fresh.

STRETCH AND GROW

Mind Stretcher Game

In a group, it is best to create a set of cards with a stretcher on each card. Pass around the deck and have each person draw three to five cards and take turns sharing their answers.

Describing myself, I am ....

Three of my passions are ....

I choose to reflect on the positive when ....

I felt supported when ....

I saw beauty in ....

I believe in myself when ....

My high this week was ....

I found myself listening when ....

I see my next step as ....

I felt compassion when............

I saw wisdom when ....

I am proud of ....

I am thankful for ....

I notice I am blessed when ....

A good childhood memory ....

I am good at ....

One of my hopes or desires is..............

When I have free time, I love to ....

I saw a miracle when ....

Three people who have influenced me are ...., because........

Two decisions I made that changed my life are .....

A major event in my life was ....

Food For Thought

These cards have helped me for years, and still do today. If I have a bad day, I would pick the card that speaks to me, I would put it some place I could see it with ease as a reminder and thought adjuster.

So, whenever you have a thought that does not serve you, go to these cards. Start repeating the one that calls to you until you find yourself with better thoughts.

Food For Thought Cards:

If you always do, what you have always done, you will always get what you have always got.

I forgive myself forever doubting my wisdom

Everything is working out for the highest good for everyone concerned

Example:

Let's say my car broke down and I think there is no money to fix it. I would be bombarded with negative thoughts. When that happens, I would grab my cards and pick one to help me. I would go for a walk or sit quietly with the intention to keep my thoughts open for a positive outcome. Repeating and memorizing the card allows me to empty my cup of fear, doubt and worry. If I do this for 10 minutes, I have stayed positive for that time which helps me become open to solutions or alternatives. Anytime I can stay positive for a period of time, I will always feel better which clears my mind.

Editor's Note: "I AM" are two of the most powerful words we can ever say and anything that follows it will manifest. This is a game that you can use with children to help them with their self-esteem.

2001   *UP YOUR ENERGY*

I Am

You can use this game to shift energy into a more positive way of being at any time. As you use these statements, also make a list of each one to review over time as situations come up.

Examples: I AM strong when ....

I AM strong when I stay peaceful in traffic. I AM strong when my children want their own way. I AM strong when I become still and visualize my desire.

I AM strong when ....

I AM peaceful when.............

I AM powerful when ....

I AM kind when ....

I AM honest when.................

I AM patient when ....

I AM learning when...................

Editor's Note: Words are the way we communicate everywhere we go. The more powerful the words, the more successful you are. It becomes easier to communicate with others and be understood. People seem to think that women talk more than men. In an article in Scientific American July 2007 it was discovered "...the sexes came out just about even in the daily averages: women at 16,215 words and men at 15,669."*

2001   *SUCCESSFUL PEOPLE*

Power Words

Power words are a wonderful gift you give to yourself or family. Create a list of positive words, or attributes that will enhance your living such as confidence, focus, or courage. Make a deck of cards for the game by putting one word on each card. Using power words daily will help you to increase moral-fiber or reinforce the words you already use. With Power Word Cards I have used them in two ways. In a group, have each person pick a card and use in a positive sentence. Let us say I picked "Strength," you could say "I used strength when I finished my chores for the day." Do a few a day and find out what your subconscious is really thinking.

Another way of using Power Words is to pick three cards from the deck you have created. Let's say you picked these three words: Blessed, Loved, and Understanding. Now write a sentence i.e., I am Blessed to feel Love and be Understood.

Here is a list of examples to get you started. Please add your own on the bottom.

Abundance	Accept
Create	Learn
Feelings	Appreciated
Inspired	Creative
Awesome	Beautiful
Interest	Blissful
Compassionate	Courageous
Imagination	Clarity
Cheerful	Excited
Energized	Delighted
Determined	Creative
Enthusiastic	Confident
Determined	Calm

Empowered	Peaceful
Loving	Fantastic

*Gender Jabber: Do Women Talk More than Men?

In a word: No. But then, how did the rumor get started?

By Nikhil Swaminathan

Editor's Notes: This is the best way I know to have my friends and family remind me of what I am saying. We are often so busy talking we forget to filter or modify what is coming out of our mouths. Every time I hear a bell it causes me to stop and review not only what I say but what I am thinking as well.

2001   *DING-A-LING*

The Bells

In a group and when alone, put small bells within arm's reach. You will be hearing the bell when you least expect it, giving you a new awareness. Playing this game allows you to step out of the way and learn new ways to use your words wisely.

There are unconscious sentences we say on a daily basis that do us no good. They stop the flow of our growth. By playing the bell game, we have an opportunity to readjust our thoughts into a more positive action. This leads the group to share new ways that create better outcomes.

Let us say that I came to the Power Circle in the

dumps. I feel the need to share that, but how could I say it in a positive way, to get my point across?

I could say, "Today was a very hard day." The bells would ring. Hard is a word that stops us in our tracks, creating a wall to climb. What if you said: "I know that tomorrow will be a much better day than today." Here you have spoken a new truth putting action in a positive direction for tomorrow. If this sentence becomes a loop in your thinking, it will be working for you in the future. Here is another, "I can't find a job." The bells begin to ring. This is a negative thought you do not want to happen. What is it you desire? "I know I will be finding a job soon, I can feel it in my bones." In this way, you have a brighter outlook and the listener knows you are looking for a job to come your way.

"I was sitting in a hot truck waiting for someone for hours." The bells ring. This is negative because it tells us the truck was hot and you were upset. You could say, "I was grateful for the breeze by having the windows down as I sat in the truck." In this way, the listeners can hear your wisdom and still know it was a hot day.

Create cards with daily negative sentences so that your group can give new positive options. I have offered you a starting point. Take this time to turn each of these negative thoughts into a more positive thought.

Activity: Rewrite these sentences to be more powerful.

Boy, last year I worked so hard that I didn't take any vacation.

I hate my picture taken, I take horrible photos.

Something always bad happens to me on a trip

I never can keep up with the housework

I am so unlucky

We always get lost when going to a new address.

I had a crappy day

I had a crappy day! This would be your truth, yes, but saying it out loud or to yourself, you are now creating more "crappy" to come to you.

Take the time to discuss how you could tell the group you had a crappy day, without causing it to create more crappy days. The group will get it and you have stayed positive.

Have your group take turns sharing the cards to make it fun and interesting, have a few of your own positive and negative thoughts included. This exercise is to learn to distinguish between a positive thought and a negative thought as you hear the bells to remind you to be more positive. To make the game more exciting, have positive and negative thoughts included in the deck.

Children are the fastest ones to ring the bell. I found they listen closely to our every word. If they hear one of us say that something was hard. They ring the bell. When I am working with someone and I hear them put themselves down, I verbally ring the bell and have them come up with an alternate statement. Play this game with your family or friends at home or at work. Tell them to ring the bell on you if they think they hear a negative sentence coming out of your mouth. Then take the time to rephrase it.

Editor's Afterword

"Discovering Your True Brilliance" has been a work of love for Sheila over several years. She continues to work with men, women and children to guide them in ways to enjoy a high energy, peaceful, successful life.

There is no age limit to making positive changes in one's life. I have used the tools and continue to use them. When I do, I notice great positive changes taking place for me.

CPSIA information can be obtained at www.ICGtesting.com
Printed in the USA
BVOW082352010413

317006BV00001B/4/P

9 781452 568843